I JUST WANT TO BE HAPPY!

Six Steps to Living Your Best Life

by

Debbie Pearson

Mindset and Self-Discovery Coach

DEBBIE PEARSON

I Just Want to Be Happy!

© Debbie Pearson, 2019

All rights reserved. No part of this book may be reproduced in any form without permission in writing from the author. Reviewers may quote brief passages in reviews.

No part of this publication may be reproduced or transmitted in any form or by any means, mechanical or electronic, including photocopying or recording, or by any information storage and retrieval system, or transmitted by email without permission in writing from the author.

Neither the author nor the publisher assumes any responsibility for errors, omissions, or contrary interpretations of the subject matter herein. Any perceived slight of any individual or organization is purely unintentional. Throughout this book the author has used examples from many of her clients' personal lives. However, to ensure privacy and confidentiality, she has changed their names and details of their experience. None of the personal examples of the author's own life have been altered. The author is not a therapist or mental health professional. Readers are advised to seek professionals for treatment.

Brand and product names are trademarks or registered trademarks of their respective owners.

Design: Deb Pearson, LLC
Editing: Laurie Ann Ellis
Author photo: S. A. Melancon

Published by Deb Pearson, LLC
Email: Deb@DebbiePearson.com
Website: www.DebbiePearson.com

*For every wounded inner child,
this book was written for you.*

Contents

Contents
Introduction
1 - What Did I Ever Do to Deserve This?
2 - Fat Green Peas
3 - Why Take the Red Pill?
4 - Who Are You Today?
5 - Wise Choices
6 - If I Have to Do It, Why Doesn't He?
7 - Be Unstoppable For Yourself
8 - No More Locked Rooms
9 - Four Steps to Keep Moving Forward
10 - Is Today the Day?
11 - This Is The End (but not really)

Acquired Information

Acknowledgments

References

About the Author

Thank You Page

INTRODUCTION

"P.S. Tell my brother and sister I love them."

Those were the last words I wrote in the note to my parents, just before climbing out of my bedroom window to run away from home. It was just two weeks before the end of my high school senior year. I didn't care. I hated every aspect of my life and couldn't take living at home anymore. After walking for nearly an hour loaded down with clothes, zI found a payphone (there weren't cell phones back then) and called Charlie, a biker I had met at the Lakefront about 5 months earlier who I had started dating. He came to pick me up, and I went to live with him, a 35 year-old man, as his 17 year-old girlfriend.

Living with Charlie opened my eyes to an entirely different world. New to my life were bikers, and rowdy loudmouths, and guns with bullets that would sometimes go off. Once a bullet flew so close to my head my hair moved. There was quite a bit of drinking and drug use, laughing about nothing, and having sex with different people. Also new to my life was a feeling of belonging. I felt a sense that I mattered, what I said had impact, and people seemed to enjoy having me around. It was Was this happiness?

My home life had been nothing like this. I wasn't sure I belonged. I felt left out. What I said or wanted didn't seem to matter; I didn't seem to matter. Only what my dad wanted mattered. Up until now I had been living in a state of numbness, but living at Charlie's and having the drugs, allowed the numbness to take a backseat. I had never laughed that much, never had alcohol or drugs, nor had I known about hanging out in bars or riding motorcycles. And I never knew the affections of a man before. I found I enjoyed all of it. The best part about this phase of my life was the attention, especially the male attention. I desperately needed it and hearing how wonderful I was made me feel special.

Life was crazy amazing - for a while. After three months, Charlie's ex-girlfriend decided she still loved him and showed up on his doorstep. Charlie didn't know she was coming back, until she appeared. We called her Buggy Brenda because she was a little on the crazy side. About a week after being back in the house, Brenda decided she'd had about enough of another female being there. After a long evening of valium, quaaludes, marijuana and drinking, Buggy Brenda went to the kitchen, opened the drawer, pulled out a knife, put it behind her back, and with a sly smile on her face walked over to me. She lifted the shiny, sharp metal and held it to my throat. My eyes widened; I stopped breathing. I could feel the cold steal against my skin, but I couldn't move. My heart pounded in my ears. As she threatened to slit my throat, Charlie grabbed her hand and pulled it back, gently pried open her fingers, taking away the knife. He was enjoying this. He smiled at her, his eyes excitedly dancing back and forth between hers cooing, "It's not a full moon, darling. I don't think it's a good night for blood, do you?" Still holding her eye, he bent down, gently kissed her lips and asked if she wanted something to drink. Shock coursed through me. Did he just do that? Did that just happen? Now terrified, I called a friend (from the landline) to come pick me up at the corner grocery 3 blocks away. I ran down the street as fast as I could. This was definitely not happiness.

I ended up back at my parents' house that night – it was safer than being around Buggy Brenda – but I knew I couldn't stay there long. I took summer classes and ended up with a G.E.D. In desperation, I joined the Army to again get away. During Basic Training I injured my knee in an exercise. In an unusual case, I was discharged after serving only seven months. Where was there to go? Back to my parents' house.

As if I had never left, the tension between my dad and I was still high. He seemed intent on belittling me, ignoring me, or speaking "at" me. His voice bellowed in nasty, loud, and demeaning tones. He looked at me with disdain, his nose always tilted up with that slight wrinkle of disgust. He walked past me in a puffed up posture as if to say "this is my space and you don't belong". All the reasons I had left in the first place were still palpable and I was miserable. I got 2 jobs and as quickly as possible rented a cheap apartment and got the hell out of there.

My search for happiness continued. Surely, living on earth was not about misery, frustration, boring conversation, suffering through it all. Or was it? I could not seem to find a way to feel happiness other than here and there when the circumstances seemed just right.

A few years later, when I was 24 years old, my friend Nohemy invited me to attend something called *The Growth Workshop*. This experience opened my eyes to new possibilities. I was learning healthy information and it was helping me feel better about myself and about life. It gave me hope that there is a way to find happiness after all. I found myself continuing to search for that little piece of magic that would calm down the feelings of unworthiness, anger and self-doubt.

I spent decades trying to figure out how to get rid of the emotional pain from childhood. I participated in women's circles, sat on therapists' couches, and had many late-night telephone calls with friends. I read self-help and spiritual books, attended awareness-raising workshops, watched motivational videos, and participated in webinars and courses. My life and outlook were getting increasingly better, but still, the emotional pain persisted.

Along the way, I shared stories with my friends about what I was learning and how to apply the lessons not only to my life, but to theirs as well. I often heard that I should write a book. Writing was never something that interested me. I love art, especially painting, but writing? No way.

Years went by and I learned more and more about emotional pain and abuse during childhood, and how to move through it. I worked with a lot of experts trying different techniques and methods and putting them to the test. I began to specialize in self-care, personal development and self-knowing. Over and over I continued to hear, "You should write a book," but I didn't really want to write about that kind of stuff, or anything else for that matter.

As I look back, I can see that during my life I was depressed in the way where I functioned fully during the day, would laugh with others, hang out, participate in activities occasionally, but also that I drank a little too much each night to cope with my dissatisfaction, sadness, and feelings that I just wasn't *enough*. This had to change. I was 56 years old and still doing the same things every day, expecting change.

This book is about the steps I took to transform my life. I've gone from frustrated, angry, unfulfilled, surviving, existing and getting through each day not even knowing why I'm here, to feeling genuine happiness, worthy of having a wonderful life, being able to validate why I'm here, realizing that I am enough as I am, and that I deserve to be happy {birthright}.

My hope for you is that the contents of this book can bring change to your life and help you start down the road of self-fulfillment, self-caring, self-appreciation, self-worth, self-compassion, and more. It is not only possible; it is probable with the willingness and daring to learn new things and to do things differently. To be brave enough to look for your voice. To be in enough wonderment to embrace your inner child. To have the guts to stand up for yourself. Many of us have been successful in our lives in a number of ways and still struggle to feel worthy. Some of us have found our way through the struggle. Is it time for you to find your way? You don't have to go it alone.

I've been told numerous times, "I learned more from you in

just 6 months than I learned in 20 years of therapy." Now that was someone who coached with me, but if you'd like to dip your toe in for free, please feel free to join the Self-Discovery Lab, a private women-only Facebook group. We'd love to have you.

1
What Did I Ever Do to Deserve This?

My life ended up being one of shame, guilt, anger, low self-esteem, and self-hate.

I have often wondered why some people have kind, compassionate, caring dads and why mine was always so mean to me. Do you have a parent that treats you badly? If you do or did, my inner child is reaching out to hold hands with and hug your inner child. From the time I was born, my dad treated me like crap. It was as if he hated me and I don't know what I ever did for him to have that type of behavior toward me.

The words he used, the tone of his voice, the actions he took, the abandonment, the looks of hate, the belt beatings I got—all left me with feelings of extreme unworthiness. My life quickly spun into a place of complete and total numbness. Try as I might, I never figured out what I did to deserve such treatment. What about you? If your life was anything like mine, my heart already hurts for you.

My life ended up being one of shame, guilt, anger, low self-esteem, and self-hate. I grew up never feeling comfortable anywhere, often feeling like an outcast, and wondering why I never felt as if I measured up. I desperately wanted to fit in and would try wearing the same types of clothing as others wore, try speaking their lingo, or try dating guys I thought others who were important would approve of, but even when I was allowed into a group, it seemed as if they would find me a little too different, and, again, I'd be ignored or ostracized, and the low self-esteem would rear its ugly head.

My heart hurt. I was confused. My life sucked. I saw myself as a loser and wondered who would want to be friends with me? I did not feel worthy of being loved. And this made for a lonely and sad life.

As I got older, I began to look for ways to understand why my life was the way it was. I went to therapy and devoured many self-help books. I began to understand more and started making some changes in my life. A little here and a small change there, the nuggets of insight gave me some reprieve, but overall the sad, painful experience of not feeling worthy or being enough was ever present.

I continue to look for answers, because I wanted the pain to go away. I didn't want to live with it any longer, and wondered if it would be with me forever. I mean, my dad created this mess, shouldn't he have to clean it up? Why wasn't he? Those are the rules, right? You open it, you close it. You turn it on, you turn it off. You make a mess, you clean it up. Why wasn't he cleaning up the mess he made?

I began to research how, as children, our worth is created. Growing up, we depend on our parents, and other caregivers, to give us the basic needs of survival. And somewhere, at some age, we leave our homes and move out on our own. But how is it that some of us continue to live as if we are still dependent on others to determine our worth? How is it that we allow others to determine our importance? More often than not, the information that gets downloaded into our brains on a daily basis perpetuates the feeling that we "aren't enough." Social media wreaks havoc on us by portraying the perfect family. And we believe it. But why?

Think about this. If someone says, "You're a blue lizard," you don't really have much response to that because there have been no programs downloaded into your brain about you being blue or being a lizard or about that being bad or wrong. But what happens when someone, especially someone who is supposed to love and protect you, tells you you're ugly, stupid, lazy, or worthless? If you have a reaction inside of you to any of those words, it's because on some level you believe them. Someone told you, or something happened in your life, and on some level you believed the negative statements were true.

I hated feeling this way. I wanted to find out why we go through life believing all the BS that other people tell us, and why we seem to download the negative stuff and remember it, but the positive stuff seems to get deleted, or not received, not accepted? Why do we keep just the negative and not the positive?

Even after I moved out on my own, the emotional abuse from my dad was still in my head. Even without consciously realizing it, almost everything I did was based on how I thought my dad would react to me if he knew. At thirty-five years old, married with a child and living in another state, I was still possessed with the worry or concern of what he'd think and how he'd react if he came to my house. I tried to pretend differently, but concern for what my dad would think about me was pervasive. All I wanted was to be accepted by him, hear a good word, an occasional compliment. It never came and I found I was always questioning myself and my decisions. I never felt whole. In fact, I often felt more like a child than an adult, with open emotional wounds that would not heal. I wanted to be happy, and pretended I was, but that was not the truth.

I've had people tell me that something is wrong with me. I've had people tell me I'm broken. Hearing that made me really angry. Why am I the broken one? I've had others tell me to just forgive. (Forgive? I didn't know how to do that and wasn't willing to.) Others have said I just need to forget about it and move on. How do you forget the abuse and this type of emotional pain? It's not as if wishing it to go away will make it go away. I have realized that it's easy for others to tell you what they think you should do, but that doesn't mean it's easy for you, or that you want what they want.

I didn't feel broken even though I felt as if something was wrong. I wasn't willing to forgive or forget either, at least not at that time. No, I wanted a third option. I wanted to understand what the problem was and how to fix it. I'd worry about who or what was broken, and I'd think about forgiving and forgetting later, after I'd figured out what to do with this nonstop residual emotional pain. I couldn't give up. I had to keep searching for answers.

2
Fat Green Peas

"You realize this is all your fault, right?"

My mission is to help you stop feeling like a victim and to start healing. My goal is to not just get you to the pain-free zone, but to show you how to find that deep inner, genuine happiness and life fulfilment you are searching for. But first, let me share a couple of stories from my childhood. I'm hoping that by sharing you'll see how much I understand your emotional pain. Like you, none of this was my fault, but I've come to see that it is my responsibility to figure out a better way to live life. I have found it takes great desire, courage of the heart, determination and deep inner self-discovery to work through the pain in order for it to dissipate. But, oh, how it is *worth it*.

One night, when I was seven years old, we had big, fat green peas for supper. There they were right next to the creamy, delicious white mashed potatoes and the crispy fried chicken leg. This was not the first time I'd tasted them. I knew I didn't care for them, but my dad thought I should try them again because maybe I would enjoy them *this time*. I told him I wouldn't like the taste because they still smelled the same yucky way they did last week, and I didn't like them that time either. We went back and forth a few times with him insisting I try them and me pleading my case. He had to win.

Angered, he unbuckled his belt and slid the thirty-six inch long, two-inch wide leather weapon from his belt loops and draped it over his shoulder. This was a common threat, and scary to me, because I never knew when he would use that belt. This particular day was a little different.

He glared at me, eyes narrowed, lips pursed and through clenched teeth he said, "You're going to eat one pea, dammit, just taste it."

Crying, I pleaded "Nooooo." I refused his demand, and he stood up.

The second he pushed his chair out, I knew what was coming, and I jumped out of mine. It was fight-or-flight time, and there was no way I could fight him. He chased me. Round and round the table we went, with me barely getting away, scrambling as fast as I could, until the moment he caught me. I was so scared. I was crying out for my mom, tears running down my face. He was pissed that I "disobeyed" him. His face was red and his neck veins were popping. He was angrily shouting at me that I needed to listen to him when he told me to do something.

When he grabbed me, I instinctively tried to pull away, which pissed him off even more. I pulled and yanked, terrified, desperately trying to get my arm from his grasp. In a split second, my body was down on the floor, and as quick as lightning his whole body straddled my small upper chest pinning down my shoulders and arms with his knees squeezed in tight. His weight made it hard for me to breathe.

His thumb and forefinger reached around my nose and squeezed it shut. The second I parted my lips enough to try and get in a little air, with his other hand he took one big, fat green pea and shoved it down into my mouth. I gagged and choked and cried. Satisfied that he had won, he got up off my chest and headed back to his chair.

"You realize this is all your fault, right?" he sneered, teeth clenched. "If you would've just listened and done what I told you, none of this would've happened. Now go to your room!"

What is it that makes one human treat another this way? It's a baffling proposition to try and understand. But I wanted to understand, I wanted to know. My hope was that if I understood, then maybe I'd find a way to be free of the pain, maybe I could make some sense of his actions.

My life was filled with a variety of occurrences where my dad had what I'll call an over-reaction to something that could have been handled differently, like, in a *humane* way. I felt beaten down most days of my younger life and felt like his punching bag. The above had a huge impact in my life. As children, we are at the mercy of our parents, and certain other authority figures in our lives. Here's one last story.

When I was eleven years old, I was playing with some friends in the small living room of our house. My dad walked in, and we all could tell he was upset because he was yelling. Everyone froze and stared wide-eyed as he shouted about "someone stinking with B.O."

He grabbed one boy's arm, "Is it you goddammit?" he asked angrily, then lifted and sniffed my friend's armpit. It wasn't him, so my dad moved to the next kid to the right. He grabbed the next kid's arm, lifted and sniffed. Two more kids and he got to me. He roughly grabbed my arm, lifted it in the air, and sniffed.

"It's you," he said in disgust, pushing me backward, spewing his hatred. "Get your ass in the bathroom, take a bath, and put on some goddamn deodorant. You stink!" He turned my little body around roughly and shoved me toward the hallway door. I had to catch myself from falling. I didn't understand what was happening or why he was treating me this way. What did I do? Sobbing and confused as I was pushed through the bathroom door, I turned my head around and looked up at him with questioning eyes. All I saw was his disgust as he slammed the door shut.

And, that's how I was taught it was time to use deodorant.

I could go on and on with stories about how my father seemed to enjoy embarrassing me by making fun of me, calling my friends derogatory names like fatty or stupid-ass, saying gross words or statements at supper trying to get someone to throw up, the constant threat of the belt and the beatings. I never felt safe when he was around, but I had no idea what to do. I remember thinking, "No one can save us from the monster."

Around other people he was a different person. If I said anything negative about him, most people would look at me confused and tell me I was crazy and not to talk about my father in a negative way. "Honor thy father and mother," people would drone, quoting the Bible. I often wondered why thy father and thy mother don't have to honor thee? All I knew for sure was that I was at his mercy. Being as numb as possible seemed my only hope of survival in that crazy, uncomfortable world I lived in.

I often wondered why my dad was so mean to me, but was never able to figure out what I did to deserve it. Being numb, I never even realized that other people's dads didn't treat them this way, but my dad sure did seem to enjoy making fun of me, embarrassing me, yelling at me, and putting me down in front of other people, especially my friends. In my whole life, I honestly cannot even remember one compliment coming from his mouth. Not one. Not ever. Why would a parent never compliment their child?

Even after moving out, his influence and control was in my life as I was still occasionally asking him for money. It took several years before I realized it, but eventually I saw how that continued to give him power over my decisions. Another realization was that I had not been taught to take care of myself emotionally or financially. Really, I had no real concept of who I was. It seemed that all the information I knew about myself came from other people. And mostly, I displayed characteristics others wanted me to have. Apparently, if I acted particular ways, that would make them feel better but it didn't necessarily make me feel better. I wondered if I mattered at all, anywhere?

Not knowing who I was had me looking for acceptance whenever and wherever I could find it. I spent some number of years drinking way too much alcohol, having eating issues, doing drugs, being promiscuous, hanging out with the wrong people, and finding ways to have fun just to overcome the boredom and nothingness I felt. I knew there must be more to life than pain and numbness and trying to not feel either. But what, and how? I wanted to find meaning.

Dad felt differently. He genuinely believed that he had everything figured out and that his way was the best way and that everyone (everyone that he could dominate) should acquiesce to his desires. There were more than a couple of times I heard him say, "If only people would do what I want, then everything would be better." Seriously? Better for who?

I remember this one time when my parents came to my house. I was in my forties and my dad was going to help me figure out what was wrong with my dryer. For us, that meant, I stand around watching and being quiet while he does whatever needs to be done. For all his faults, my dad was a savvy mechanic and could fix most anything. Taking apart the dryer to figure out the problem, my dad laid out a small white wash rag on top of the washing machine lid. He piled screws, nuts, washers, etc. in specific little piles so he would know exactly what order and where to put them when it was time to replace them. My mom came in with an armload of clothes and asked if she could use the washing machine. I was shocked at the extreme manner in which my dad spoke to my mom. In an explosion of hate-filled sounds and snarls he yelled, "No goddammit, you can't use the washing machine right now. I've got my tools and the parts laying just so.

Go do something else." I was a bit stunned at the level of hostility he displayed towards my mom.

As I said, this incident occurred at my house. I said to my dad, "You could have just told her no without yelling. She would have gone away with no problem." All I can tell you is that he became irrationally infuriated and walked out of the laundry room yelling something like, "... and you don't know a goddamn thing." He walked over to the radio and turned it up unnecessarily loud.

My father had always used the premise that one can do whatever they want in their own house, and in his house, everyone had to do what he wanted, or they could leave. His way or the highway. Well, okay, if that's the rule, let's go with that. This time we were in *my* house but he still tried to control.

I walked into the room and turned the radio down and calmly said, "In this house, we respect each other. Let's keep the sound at a reasonable level so we're not disturbing the others." I left the room to go back to what I was doing. He turned the radio way up again. I couldn't believe it—and yet I could. He was testing me. It was upsetting and scary, because he was forcing me to be confrontational. This was my house, and according to him when I grew up and owned my own home, I could make whatever rules I wanted. So, here we were, me with my house rules, and him completely disregarding them.

I walked back into the living room, turned the volume back down to reasonable, and again calmly said, "Dad, it's important to me that we all show each other respect. Please leave the radio at a reasonable volume. There are other people in the house." And I left the room.

In that moment, the room filled back up with even louder music. I found my heart racing. All the calm and respect I had managed to maintain vanished in an instant. Frustrated and angry, I made a bee-line to the shed and retrieved a pair of electrical wire cutters. I returned to the living room where the radio continued to blare. I pulled the plug gently from the socket, and silence ensued. However, the air was thick with tension. His eyes burned with resentment as he stared at me—challenging his authority was unthinkable to him. Holding the cord in one hand and the wire cutters in the other, I met his gaze squarely, feeling a mix of unease and righteousness.

With absolute sincerity, I said. "Don't make me cut this fucking cord."

I laid the cord down on the floor and walked out of the room, wire-cutters in hand. My heart was beating a mile a minute. I don't enjoy confrontation, but he was testing me and I had to stand up for myself. He didn't plug the cord back in, but instead walked outside. Did I just win, or will I be punished for this another time?

I've done a lot in my life to try and get approval from my dad. I'm not sure why I felt that was necessary. At some point, I turned away from trying to please him and decided that I only needed my own approval and that what my father had instilled in me daily wasn't necessarily the truth. I'm surprised at how difficult it's been.

Through many self-help seminars I've learned a lot. They've been eye-opening and rewarding, but something was always missing. I've traveled in and around the US, to Hawaii, Central America, and seven countries in Europe. I love to travel but seeing the world hasn't solved my problem either. I've had many jobs over the years, always trying to find the one that satisfied me, made me happy, fulfilled me.

Owning my art business for over a decade was certainly rewarding in the creativity realm, yet something was still missing. I wanted to feel a part of something, something bigger than myself, to somehow make a difference. I wanted to help people heal. "I" wanted to heal.

During my six years as a military civilian, I was the art specialist at the Armed Forces Retirement Home, the director of a

Skills Development Center at Keesler AFB, and then direct support for three different four-star generals at Air Mobility Command, Scott AFB. But once the newness wore off, I could tell there was something was still missing. What was it?

My determination to find out increased. I felt like I needed to make a difference and thought the best thing I could do was go on a vacation with a purpose. Maybe I'd help dig a water well in a third-world country, rescue animals, build houses for poor people, or something like that. As I searched, I eventually came across something that held my interest, so much so that everything else was forgotten. Something caught my interest in a big way.

The more I researched it, the more excited I felt. I bought a ticket, purchased the right clothes and equipment, and began physical training in order to backpack 500 miles across Spain on the path called El Camino de Santiago (aka the Camino).

In the beginning, I found myself walking the pace that others set. I'm not sure why I felt compelled to keep up with them, but I did. I let them lead the speed. I discovered that other people walk fast, way faster than is comfortable for me. This caused some problems.

About ten days in, my leg became injured. A doctor told me not to walk on it for two days, especially not carrying the weight of a backpack. All the individuals I had met walking the Camino continued on their way. They left me. I felt scared and alone. Two days in a town where I knew no one and didn't understand the language gave me a lot of time to think. I felt myself in that familiar sensation of not knowing what to do. I felt myself going numb, shutting down, thinking about quitting and going home. I didn't want that to happen, but I didn't know what else to do.

Then I saw someone I had walked with days earlier. I noticed she also had sustained an injury. She was also in pain. I shuffled toward her, and she hobbled toward me. We hugged, and we cried. We discussed what had happened to each of us. We both desperately wanted to finish. We decided to walk together, slowly.

We'd walk at our own pace. Others would pass us by, and we'd be okay with it because we realized we didn't need to compare ourselves to others. It wasn't a competition.

We chose to live according to what was going to work for us. We began to live from the inside out. What was right for us came from inside of us, instead of looking outside of ourselves for the answers. Eureka! It was the first time in my life that I felt incredible burdens lift and a freedom I never knew existed. It's what I had been looking for. We were free to determine our speed. We were free to determine how far we'd travel in a day. We were free to determine that we had as much right to go slowly as others had to go fast.

Embracing a slower pace taught me one of my most valuable lessons: the importance of prioritizing my own well-being. It's a simple yet profoundly symbolic realization. I learned that acting in my own best interest, not at the expense of others but for my personal growth, is crucial. This insight has stayed with me. By nurturing myself, I am able to offer more to those around me. This shift brought me a deep sense of inner awareness and a significant measure of happiness, even if it was fleeting.

Walking the Camino was a life-changing experience. I knew something important had happened within me, I just didn't realize how significant, impactful, and life changing it was going to be for the rest of my life). What I did know was that I was happier on the Camino than I had ever been in my life. It took me thirty-eight glorious days of walking 5-7 nature-filled hours per day. And all along the way, I learned the most amazing lessons.

Then the day arrived when I had to return to my job. The familiar weight of burden and constraint settled over me once more, leaving me feeling trapped and without purpose. Determined to reclaim control over my life, I chose to pursue a path as a Certified Coach and Trainer. The moment I received my certificate, a light ignited within me. It was as if I suddenly recalled that my true calling on this earth was to teach and inspire others.

The moment arrived when I knew it was time to leave my federal job. I decided to sell everything I owned, except for what could fit in my car. Driving away, I was overwhelmed with a fabulous sense of liberation, experiencing for the second time in my life the incredible feeling of burdens lifting and freedom sweeping in. This liberation was not about shirking responsibilities or dismissing others; it was about honoring what mattered most to me and taking responsibility for living authentically. This decision has proven to be the most rewarding of my life. Every day brings new learning and growth, deepening my love for life.

Now, I set ambitious goals with powerful intentions and strive to live with conscious awareness. I've learned effective ways to manage stress, chaos, and drama, and I embrace compassion and love as much as possible. I understand how to handle intense emotions like anger—recognizing the trigger, understanding the emotion, and knowing how to respond effectively. Feelings of anger, frustration, worthlessness, hopelessness, and helplessness no longer dominate my life.

Whether you're dealing with challenging family dynamics or personal strife, I want to share with you the insights and skills that have freed me from so much unnecessary emotional pain. This book offers key life skills essential for a joyful, fulfilling existence.

I cherish the opportunity to share this message with you, to hear your stories, and to help you discover that with the right knowledge, courage, commitment, and practice, you can achieve deep inner peace and truly love your life. Watching clients like Sara, who told me, "It's been the best three months of my life!" discover new insights and celebrate their 'aha' moments is profoundly rewarding. If you want this, you can have this, as long as you're willing to learn some new information and practice it.

You can see what it's like inside the Self-Discovery Lab. It's a free, private, women-only supportive group that explores a new topic every month. If you fit the criteria, please feel free to join us.

3
Why Take the Red Pill?

Do you think about what you think about?

The main character, Neo, was offered two pills in the movie *The Matrix*: a red one and a blue one. He needs to choose which to take. He asks Morpheus what the difference is. Morpheus tells him but then gives him the chance to decide.

If Neo takes the blue pill, he would go back to sleep, back to the life he had been living, unaware of anything beyond him, as if that's all there is. If he takes the red pill, he will undergo an awakening, his eyes will be opened to the truth, and his mind will be freed. Neo has a hard choice to make because he has to decide to either stay where it was familiar (comfort zone) or choose a complete unknown (potentially terrifying). Neo chooses to know *the truth, even though it was scary,* and took the red pill.

I have the feeling that if someone offered you a red pill and said, "If you take this pill, all of your emotional pain will go away," you would be tempted to take it, but I'm also betting you wouldn't take it. We came to earth to learn, understand, overcome hardships, and be proud of our accomplishments. In the same vein, if someone offered you a first-place ribbon to hang on your wall to show you as the top winner, you wouldn't accept it because inside, you know that it is the earning of the reward that makes it so sweet.

It is the same for not choosing a pill to make the pain go away. You want to *move through* the emotional pain. You want to prove to yourself that you can get to the pain-free zone. Maybe you disagree with me, but deep down inside, you know if you have the right information, you want to be the one who moves you to the other side. It's why most people don't want things handed to them. Getting to happiness and fulfillment is very doable, but it takes a true desire to learn what needs to be learned, and then it takes practice until it is a habit or automatic. Time is going to pass regardless of what you do or do not do; why not make your time worthwhile and valuable?

This chapter provides an overview of the book's content. The following chapters teach you various methods for shifting, changing, altering, growing, and finding more joy, happiness and fulfillment in your life. I've written this as a guide to help you work out these issues on your own. However, I'm here for you if you need or want help. We can go through this together.

Beginning to Break the Spell

Breaking the toxic spell that others have in your life will take some work, but the reward is worth it. We'll activate parts inside of you that have been asleep for a long, long time. You will find clarity, and that clarity will fuel you. How amazing do you think it will be to stop suppressing your innate need to grow and thrive and to also learn to transform old patterns and beliefs into new patterns of empowerment?

There are changes that will happen quickly; others will take some time. It's normal. The brain is wired for success, but it has been *programmed* to fail. How sad is that? I'm trying to help you understand that you can shift away from what no longer serves you and learn what you need to be successful in your own life. And that is what this book is meant to do; it's to help you learn new information, to become more aware of what has happened, and what can potentially happen in the future, should you desire it.

Here's what my client, Annabelle, said after experiencing this work:

I just want to express my deepest gratitude for this incredible and insightful information. Because of what I've learned when an uncomfortable event happens, I may feel sad, but I don't blame the other person. I'm able to see things differently. In the past, I would have tried to make the other person wrong; now, I do not. And for that, I'm eternally grateful.

For Annabelle, this revelation created a huge shift. She can experience life from a place of emotional clarity, and what happens for her now is the emotional pain that used to be prominent has become subdued. She is participating and choosing differently in life, and life is becoming softer, more gentle, more understandable, and easier to deal with.

You can do this too. You may not know it and you may not currently feel it, but you have the strength and power within you to do everything I've laid out in this book. I've gone through all of this, as have hundreds of others. You can do it on your own if you'd prefer, that's certainly possible, but I am here to support you - a little or a lot - if you want someone to give you some suggestions, hold your hand, give you a virtual hug or encouragement. You are not alone on this journey if you don't want to be.

To grow, you need to be willing to learn new and different things, especially about yourself. Albert Einstein said, "You can't solve a problem with the same mind that created it." He's a smart dude, and it's true: We can't solve problems with the same mind that created them. New information is needed.

Just as we don't notice our hair growing, we don't notice that every single time we learn something new our mind grows and expands. To come up with solutions, we must think differently, deeper, and more expansively. There might be quite a few concepts in this book that will be new and different to you, and these are the concepts that are going to make the biggest difference.

The more you use the information in this book, the more your brain will recognize this new stuff is creating positive outcomes. Wouldn't you prefer to see wonder and amazement in your life? Let the expansion begin.

But How Can Our Brains Expand?

For one thing, you can begin to think about, or pay attention to, what you think about. Most people don't pay that much attention to their thoughts, yet the human brain processes thousands and thousands of thoughts each day. It's these thoughts that make the difference between having a mediocre life and a thriving life filled with happiness and fulfillment.

Did you know that your thoughts *become the things* you are thinking of? Whether or not you're aware of it, whether or not you are conscious of it, what you think about becomes your reality. (These aren't my rules, these are the rules of quantum mechanics, quantum science and quantum physics.) We'll do an activity in Chapter 7 to give you a better sense of how this works.

Thoughts stir up all kinds of emotions. Emotions are your guidance system. They let you know if you are headed in the right direction. Emotions are the clues to let you know if what is happening is something you want more of or less of. Emotions are very important for you to pay attention to. It's easy to follow emotions you want to have. And it's good to recognize them. But, it is just as important to recognize emotions that create discomfort for you and pay even more attention to where they're coming from.

For instance, if you are happy, you want to keep moving in that direction because you want more of that. But what about anger? Does anyone ever want to be angry? Typically, we would answer no to that because we think of anger as a negative feeling. But sometimes anger is necessary, needed, and appropriate. I'm sure you can think of examples where anger is the appropriate response.

I know when I got angry enough at my childhood traumas and decided I wasn't going to take it anymore, that was an appropriate form of anger. That feeling of anger gave me positive energy to move away from what I didn't want and toward what I did want.

Self-love and Being Selfish are Two Different Things

Self-love has often been discouraged and looked down upon. It has often been considered selfish to take care of your needs. Many women, myself included, have had additional expectations placed on us by others. How dare we care for ourselves. There's laundry, cooking, cleaning, spouses, kids, homework, household chores, work, fur babies, and on and on; who has time to care for and love themselves? You do, and I do.

Self-love is an important part of keeping ourselves from getting depressed, sick, anxious, overworked, and more. I love the analogy of putting on your oxygen mask first when in an airplane because only then can you truly help others.

Finding Your North Star

Knowing the direction you are headed is so important. If you, as the captain, were sailing your sailboat from Jacksonville, Florida, to the Bermuda Triangle, do you think it would be important to know what direction you should sail? Our lives are that way too.

You'll learn about course correction, maneuvers for when the wind gets too strong, raising and lowering your proverbial sails, and other wonderful nautical challenges related to your direction. Where is your compass pointing?

Shifting One Degree at a Time

As you begin to observe your patterns and your habits, you will also begin to see how making slight, gentle, loving shifts make all the difference in getting to where you want to go. Giant ships don't turn on a dime; they slowly shift degree by degree when navigating. Turning too sharply would result in capsizing. But turning the right amount in the right amount of time allows the ship to meet its intended destination successfully and with much greater ease.

I'm inviting you to start noticing the shifts and changes

you'd like to make. It's ok to go slow, one step at a time. Do yourself a favor and be as kind, loving, compassionate, and patient as you are with your loved ones. You have the right to decide if you want to continue heading in a particular direction, or if you'd rather make a slight shift. Why? Because you matter, and what you desire in your life matters.

Making Conscious Decisions

The more you learn, the clearer it will become that you can create a life you love. As you lead yourself toward your desired life, you will not only be proud of yourself but also happy with what you've chosen because you are consciously choosing it. Becoming consciously aware is like waking up from a bad dream; it is like removing the fog from your brain.

Getting to Freedom

Educating yourself will eliminate much suffering and allow for your personal freedom. This freedom will allow for all the joy, peace, love, happiness, and fulfillment you deserve—and you deserve as much as you desire. Freedom is the point where you are able to validate yourself, know your worth, feel love for yourself, care for all of you, and know that *you are enough*; and you will not need any other person to be able to experience it.

Listen to what Stephanie had to say after taking my course, "When we become aware and start creating a foundation of true self-knowing, we really can overcome and stop being a victim to circumstances that present themselves in our lives. It's not to dismiss what we are feeling, but to acknowledge the feelings and allow them to flow in a way that is not reactive to a situation. That's where our power is and how we take it back."

I could not have said it better. When we have had enough pain from our childhood, when we're sick and tired of feeling unworthy, unlovable, and undeserving, it's time to do something about it. Somewhere, along the way, like most of us, your power was taken away from you. This book is a roadmap on how to take back your power and enjoy the personal freedom that you, as a human being, have the right to experience.

4
Who Are You Today?

I wondered, "Who am I?"

Have you ever had a moment when what you've always believed in, followed, and accepted suddenly didn't seem to make sense? A moment when you realized that other well-meaning people had been making decisions for you about what you should or shouldn't do or think and how you should or shouldn't behave... and that no one seemed to take you into account?

Can you imagine how that affects us as individuals? We are required to follow the rules of our home, our school, and teachers, and currently, the rules of the place where we work. We're taught to look outside of ourselves to see what other people want and need from us. We're not taught how to look inside of ourselves

I had a client who took a course I was teaching called "Learning to Love." when we first started, I asked all the students what they wanted to get out of this course. Her response stuck with me because she said something like, "I want to give myself all the patience, kindness, love, and forgiveness that I've been giving to others for decades."

I get it. Many of us know how to love another but fail miserably in how to love ourselves. This is one of the reasons why I highly encourage you to learn about yourself from a place of your true authenticity, as opposed to the person you've been taught to be.

So, what might that look like? Getting to know yourself

deeply would mean being clear about your values, character traits, biases, and needs.

The clearer you know yourself and accept all of your delicious little inconsistencies, quirks, foibles, and peculiarities, the happier you will be. According to Forbes, over 85 percent of people who said they knew themselves, didn't. Only 15 percent of those tested were deeply aware of themselves. Having clarity of both your strengths and weaknesses is beneficial to all areas of your life in this way, you get to see what you want to keep and what is serving you, versus what you'd rather shift away from because it no longer serves you.

The Uniqueness of You

Even though all snowflakes are snowflakes, they are all different. The same holds true for signatures and fingerprints: they are the same and yet different. We are all humans, but we are all different. What's unique about you?

I was well into my fifties and still wondering why I always felt so different from just about everyone else. I wondered why so many people seemed to get along and enjoy each other's company, but I never felt all that comfortable. It was quite uncomfortable for me, and although I spent years trying to figure it out, it wasn't until I took a personality assessment and found out more about myself that certain information was revealed to me about who I am from birth. It was quite an enlightening experience.

Where I used to think of myself as odd, weird, unwanted, an outcast, different, and other seemingly negative words, I began to realize that I'm a different *type* of person, and it started making sense that I am as different (aka rare) as I am, and now I love that about myself. I remember the warm fuzzy that went through my body when I read certain criteria that put so much into perspective. It was the clear recognition that I came into this world different; I'm supposed to be different, and suddenly I appreciated my "weirdness". I'm wondering what relief you may feel if you discover something about yourself that suddenly made certain parts of your life make sense.

You, in Black and White

One of the best ways to get to know yourself is by taking the time to discover more about yourself. You can do this through a myriad of choices, but if you want to follow what I teach in one of my most popular courses, you may want to download the Personal Profile Tool at www.DebbiesFreebies.com. The Personal Profile Tool can be used to gather your information all in one place and to look for interacting patterns. It's not about judging yourself. It's about seeing where you are, what you enjoy and want to keep, and what you don't enjoy and prefer to change or shift away from.

Since many of us have conformed to the wishes of authority figures in life, you may not realize how much you have negated or squashed certain character traits that you were born with. Physical aspects such as the shape of your hands, the texture of your hair, and the way you walk are easy to see, but there are also nonphysical aspects that are unique to you as absolutely as the physical ones are. What are your unique nonphysical traits? How can they help you become clearer about the unique individual you are?

There's also your core values, your operating system, temperament, whether you are task-oriented or people-oriented, and more. Because you spent decades listening to and learning from your parents, other authorities, social dictates and norms, your friends, social media, and so forth, you may have tried to act, dress, or pretend to be similar to others to feel accepted and feel part of that tribe. But what often happens is we forget and ignore more and more of ourselves in order to fit in, lest we experience some form of shame. Essentially, we lose, cover, shift, subdue, and hide valuable parts of ourselves. Are you experiencing a yearning for parts of you that are longing to be seen?

Trying to be what other people want you to be can make you feel diminished, and that's just a prescription for victimization and shame. We can never be what other people want us to be. Maybe a little here and a little there, but certainly not all the time and not to everyone. What I teach my students is to learn about themselves, deeply, completely, lovingly, and with kindness and compassion. You can learn and grow to be yourself unapologetically because you do not need to apologize for who you truly are. It may be what you were taught, but you do not need to live that way.

About 2,500 years ago the philosopher Socrates uttered two important words, "Know thyself," and it is just as true today as it was back then. Know *thyself*—not who your parents think you should be, not who you try to be when with friends, not who you may think you are, but who you are as the special, unique, wonderful person that you were born to be—in other words, know your true, authentic self. Going deeper and knowing more of who you are without outside influence allows you to see that you are a whole, unique, special individual and not just the culmination of other people's decisions about who they think you "should" be.

There are traits and values that you have that are completely different from others, and theirs are different from yours. What might happen if you embraced your special qualities?

Assessing Your Personal Values

Let's dig into one aspect of the Personal Profile Tool that affects all areas of our lives. Are you familiar with your personal values, also called core values? Core values are fundamental beliefs and guiding principles that dictate how a person acts according to what is important to them. If you know your core values, there's a space to write them on the Personal Profile Tool. If not, finding out what they are may be a surprise to you. I've had a number of students and clients who couldn't name their core values but could tell you what it felt like when one of their core values was crossed or violated. Knowing what your core values are gives you leverage. Let's look at what happened to Linda.

Linda was a single mom who owned a home with three young children. It was challenging for her to come up with the mortgage each month. Out of fear she would lose her house, Linda quickly took on a roommate to bring in extra cash. At first, there was a sense of relief. Linda was able to easily make the mortgage payment and felt she had made the right move.

But, the new roommate turned out to be a poor match for Linda and her family. Linda found herself having to ask for the rent check each month, which was very frustrating for her. The roommate not only didn't keep her own area clean but her stuff often spilled out into other areas of the house. Where Linda insisted her children clean up behind themselves, put their personal items in their rooms, and be respectful of house rules, the roommate didn't feel this applied to her. Linda often found herself feeling angry and annoyed, which contributed to excess strife within the household, and unfortunately, the children often paid the price.

What might have happened if Linda had been aware of her core values and had discussed them with the potential roommate prior to signing the lease? For Linda, she didn't know what her core values were, so that wasn't even a possibility. She ended up doing what so many of us do when we aren't clear about who we are .... We behave, do, and speak from a place of fear.

As Linda worked together, she discovered her top three core values were financial security, cleanliness, and respect. Now that she was consciously aware, we worked on putting together a list of important guidelines that she wanted in a good roommate. Realizing how much more peaceful, calm and happy her home could be, Linda decided to give notice to this roommate. In short order, Linda found a much better suited choice who was able to move in without Linda even missing a month of rent. She has since reported how much happier her household is.

It may not seem like it but being aware of your core values gives insight into feelings you may be having that seem to come out of nowhere. Let's look at a very small sample of core values. Do you find yourself drawn to any of these?

Dependability	Authenticity	Loyalty
Integrity	Mindfulness	Fairness
Honesty	Respect	Consistency
Efficiency	Passion	Optimism
Equanimity	Innovation	Creativity
Service	Good humor	Adventure
Compassion	Approachability	Boldness
Exploration	Motivation	Mastery
Positivity	Timeliness	Privacy
Resolution	Efficiency	Fitness
Flexibility	Courage	Precision

If not, that's ok, as there are many. As you discover your core values, choose your top three and write them on the Personal Profile Tool. Once you name them, notice how often they appear in your life and how you navigate this world according to your awareness of them.

Love Languages

Although I don't formally teach Love Languages, they seem to show up quite often in sessions with clients. Dr. Gary Chapman wrote the book *The 5 Love Languages* and has created a free online assessment (www.5lovelanguages.com), which I highly recommend and encourage you to take. There are 5 different ones. Here they are, in no particular order: acts of service, quality time, gifts, physical touch, and words of affirmation. Do you resonate with any of these?

Learning the love languages has been quite an eye-opener for many people I've worked with. When we can see that we give love according to our love language, it makes it easier to see that others give love in *their* love language. We can recognize that another person's love language is not necessarily our love language. We can broaden our awareness of how often we may be offered love but do not recognize it as love and may, therefore, deny it exists. We can experience how another may give love, even if it's not our preferred way of receiving love.

Cassandra's top three love languages are quality time, acts of service, and words of affirmation. She loves being in small, intimate groups and having deep, meaningful conversations. If she gets sick, she feels loved when someone does her chores for her. And, similar to many of us, she craves the words that tell her she is important. Cassandra is also an introvert. Her extroverted dad, on the other hand, has gifts and physical touch as his love languages—complete opposites.

Because Cassandra and her dad never got along, she thought he hated her. He was constantly trying to get her to participate in big group events, be outgoing, shake hands or hug people, and get little gifts for others to show she cared. None of that ever felt comfortable to her, and she couldn't understand why he always pushed her so hard in that direction. Sometimes her dad would buy her something, but to Cassandra, who could care less about gifts, felt as if he were trying to buy her off, and she found herself rejecting his gifts … and him.

Because they each have different love languages, the mismatch created misunderstanding and much emotional pain to the point that they both feel the other is against them. Once Cassandra understood about the love languages, her life became a lot less painful. She understood and realized that his love languages were like a foreign language she needed to learn..

Acquiring this new information made a big difference in her relationship with her father. When he gives her a gift, she can now see it's his way of showing her love, even if it's not her preferred way of receiving love, it's still a loving act.

My hope for you is to grow and expand your understanding a little more and hopefully relieve some of your emotional pain.

Can You Take Out Time For Yourself?

Some call it personal time, I call it "me-time". Earlier in my life, I felt there was not enough time in the day to have any me-time, and I found myself frustrated and irritated. Little by little

I began incorporating some me-time into my schedule and, wow, the difference was amazing. As I begin adding what makes me happy into my life, I was able to share my internal happiness.

How do you suppose one would go about finding more time for themselves? You schedule it on your calendar. Make it as important as an appointment with your doctor or lawyer. Whether you enjoy drawing, painting, dancing or singing, gardening, cooking, meditating, chopping motorcycles, making musical instruments, putting together outfits, styling hair, reading, visualizing, watching the weather, creating forms, fluffing furniture, soaking in a tub, surfing the net, walking, running, hiking, finding creative ways to solve problems, or any other way you can think of where you find "happy-in-your-heart" is me-time. It's not about expecting others to see how busy you are and coming to your rescue. It's about you finding ways to make you happy, scheduling time on your calendar, and honoring that time. .

Spend time doing whatever you want to do, even if it's for fifteen minutes a day. Think about ways you incorporate me-time into your life, and how often you do it. Are you satisfied or do you look for more? Do you need to schedule additional time on your calendar? If you aren't scheduling enough personal time, I invite you to find creative ways to make that happen.

Take Jessica, a single mom. She didn't realize how important creativity was to her. When did, however, notice when she got home from work, she found herself being snarky to her two little ones. She knew it wasn't fair to them, but she couldn't seem to help herself. She worked a full day, and as soon as she came home, she had to cook, help with homework, prep for the next day, bathe little ones, get household chores done, and prepare everyone for bedtime. Jessica had no time for herself, and she was miserable.

In one of our coaching sessions, she blurted out, "I just need to create something!" She paused a moment and apologized for behavior. I thought it was the perfect thing that needed to happen.

Jessica was informing Jessica. We discussed various options and came up with a plan. What she ended up doing was asking her boss if she could take only thirty minutes for lunch instead of sixty, so she could leave 30 minutes earlier. That way, when she got home, she could have a little time to herself before anyone else got there. That thirty minutes has made all the difference in the world to her. She has calmed down, is no longer so grumpy with the kids, and feels so much happier. And all it took was some creative problem solving.

Will it be the same for you? Scientifically speaking, we must have some self-care and self-love that we give to ourselves. It helps with increased productivity, self-discovery, better cognitive processing, self-connecting, improved concentration, and more. Add in what your me-time is, or what you want it to be, on the Personal Profile Tool. Maybe you'll need to do some brainstorming with a friend to come up with creative ways to get what your inner child, your soul, is craving, but that's ok, do it. Hanging with a good friend could also be considered part of your me-time. Cool combo, eh?

TAKEAWAYS:

- Deep knowing of your core values gives you leverage.
- Discovering your own love language will open the door to awareness of how you express love and how others do, as well.
- Me-time, or personal time, is a human need. You matter as much as everyone else.

Feel free to join us in the Self-Discovery Lab, our private, women-only Facebook group! It's a wonderful space where you can connect, learn, and find support among other like-minded women. Since you're reading this book, we'd love to welcome you to our community!

5
Wise Choices

The words you speak matter. The actions you take matter. Choose wisely.

Christopher was sixteen. His parents were divorced but amicable. During a weekend at his dad's house, Christopher talked to his dad about needing a new computer for school. His dad suggested they go to a few different stores and see what was out there. Christopher was happy to shop for computers with his dad because it was one of the few subjects they could easily connect on. It was in third store they went to, where Chris found the perfect computer for his school needs and within a reasonable price range.

Nothing was purchased that day, but that was normal for Christopher's dad because he was frugal and wanted to check out his options before buying. Also, Chris's birthday was the following month, and his dad had given a few hints that he would get a new computer for his birthday. Christopher was excited.

"Hey, Mom, Dad's going to get me a new computer for my birthday," Chris said.

"That's wonderful, honey," his mom, Gina, replied.

When his birthday came, Christopher's dad gave him a present. The wrapped package was the right size, shape, and weight. Chris hoped it was the computer he had shown the most interest in.

That day, Chris returned home from his dad's earlier than

usual. He looked a little upset and his mom was surprised to see him.

"Everything okay?" Gina asked.

"Mom, remember I told you that Dad and I went shopping for new computers last month and that Dad had asked which one was best for school?" Christopher asked.

Gina looked up at Chris. She had a feeling this wasn't going to be good. She nodded yes to Chris as she tried to smile.

"Well, Dad did buy that new computer, the one I liked. But instead of giving it to me, he decided to keep it for himself, and gave me his old computer instead."

Gina felt that familiar sensation of frustration rush through her. Her ex-husband's lack of integrity had often been a source of irritation. He would speak in a certain way, leading her to believe one course of action, and then do something different, always justifying why it made sense to him, but not registering the negative impact it had on others.

Gina called her ex-husband to ask why he would take Christopher shopping under the guise of buying a new computer for their son only to keep the new computer—the one that Chris expressly indicated he liked—and give Chris his old one.

Christopher's dad responded, "I said I was getting him a new computer, and the one I gave him as a present is new to him. I never said the one I was buying was the one he was getting."

"Then why take him shopping and ask him which one he liked best? And why indicate he would be getting the new computer for his birthday?" Gina asked.

Disregarding the actual question, he answered, "Well, he can use the new computer anytime he comes to visit."

It All Matters

That is an example of someone having a lack of integrity. There was deceit in a few different areas, justification of his actions, immaturity, and irresponsibility. Nothing was an out-and-out lie, but nothing was quite the way it seemed either. This dad used ambiguous language to get what he wanted without considering the consequence of his words or actions, especially to his son. I'm sure it's obvious this type of behavior did not make Christopher want to participate more with his dad, but less. The words you speak matter. The way they are understood matter. The actions you take matter.

Why do people prefer dealing with a person of integrity? Because they know they can trust you to be reliable, that there will be no deceit or trickery. Having integrity means you are truthful and respectful, not only to others, but to yourself as well. If you tell someone (especially yourself) that you are going to do something, make sure you do it. I know I don't care for the way it feels when someone tells me they are going to do something and they don't; therefore, I prefer dealing with people who have integrity, and I make sure to keep my integrity intact as well.

What level of integrity shows in your actions? This means you do the right thing, because it is the right thing to do, regardless if others are watching or not. You can deceive others, but you cannot deceive yourself. You can justify your actions to others and make a case for doing what you did (also called an excuse), but deep down inside you know the truth. You know if what you're doing is right or if you are justifying. If someone throws trash out the car window but no one is watching, did the trash not get thrown? Of course it did. That person can't pretend it doesn't matter, because *all* of our actions matter, whether someone is watching or not.

If you are doing the best you can, then isn't that the best you can do? Having integrity is living in a way where you do the best you can in that given moment with the information you have. You weigh your options and make a decision. There always exists the possibility of receiving additional information, and you may end up having to make a different choice, but in that specific given moment of making the choice you do the best you can, with what you've got, from where you are. And you hold your head high knowing you did the best you could do with the information you had. Living in this beautiful space enables you to live without regrets. Can you imagine the pressure and emotional angst this one shift will alleviate?

The Thoughts We Think Matter

Maybe you already know that it's a scientific fact that your thinking plays a major role in what will happen in your life. However, if this is new to you, just allow this concept to sink in and in time it will make sense. When is the last time you really listened to the words you speak? When's the last time you really paid attention to the thoughts you think, or the actions you perform? So much of what we do (about 95% according to the National Institutes of Health) we do on autopilot.

We may realize we skip breakfast, drink coffee at certain times, prefer raspberries to strawberries, etc. but when it comes to patterns, behaviors and habits we're much less inclined to need to pay attention. When's the last time you needed to think about how to brush your teeth, how to read words (like these), or how to fry an egg, or sign your name? All these types of patterns, habits, and behaviors are stored in appropriate memory centers of our brain. Overall, it's a beautiful thing, but sometimes automatic behaviors and thoughts can cause problems.

The mind thinks somewhere between 60,000 and 80,000 thoughts per day. Assuming eight hours for sleep and sixteen hours awake, that means the mind averages in the neighborhood of 3,750 to 5,000 thoughts *per hour*. That's a lot of thoughts. To master your thoughts, you must first master your beliefs. Beliefs are what create thoughts, and thoughts reinforce beliefs. I learned that we can change our thoughts, which change our beliefs. When I learned this, it blew me away. It takes a while to really understand what this means and the impact it can have, because most of us have never been taught to look at it this way. Taking stock of our thoughts is the only way to change the ones we don't like. Here's what Jenn said about how changing her thoughts led to her changing her beliefs:

> "After yesterday's session I was able to see that I don't like how I am with my daughter. I move around quickly, always juggling several things, and she is a slow, steady mover. When I don't see her moving as quickly as I think she should, I start fussing at her to hurry up, go faster, get moving, speed it up. After you helped me see certain pattern I have, I can participate with her differently. Like, yesterday evening, while my daughter was eating supper, I wanted to tell her to hurry because we had somewhere to go. It was the perfect time to try what I learned which was to observe my beliefs about her. Instead of fussing at her, I told her the time we needed to leave. Then, I left the room. I didn't impose my stress on her. Amazingly, when it was time for us to go, she was ready and waiting on me. That blew me away, but what happened next was the real mind blower. In the car, unprompted, she thanked me for not fussing at her to hurry up. That's like a miracle for us. All I can say is, this stuff works!"

The small change of noticing her own thoughts made a huge difference in both of their lives. Learning something new like this, and practicing it, allows for the possibility of better connections in your relationships. When we don't make a shift we continue to experience emotional pain, sadness, discomfort, and often, feelings of being a victim. Observing and understanding our thoughts and beliefs helps to see where a shift might occur. Maybe, like Jenn, you might change or shift one little thought, or do something slightly different, and experience a change that pleases you.

Little Shifts + Small Steps + More Small Steps
= Big Positive Changes

Our beliefs can be so strong that we've convinced ourselves they are truths, but that's not necessarily so. Even if someone believes something with all their heart, a belief is still a belief. It may be completely and utterly true *for them*, and for lots of people they know, but it's still a belief. If it is not true for every single person on the planet, it's a belief that has become an assumption of truth. This doesn't make anyone right or wrong, that's not the point of this. What I want you to see is the difference, and that just because we *call* something a truth, doesn't make it true for another.

Some beliefs are hard to recognize, but you can discover your 'sneaky' beliefs by paying attention to your thoughts and unexamined assumptions. This is a crucial component. How we know something is true is that it applies to everyone, everywhere, all the time, exactly the same. For example, gravity, electricity, fire, water, and hours in the day. They hold the same truth for everyone, regardless of beliefs, gender, politics, biases, ethnicity, age, etc.

You may think your thoughts are *observations* about your reality, but they've actually helped *create* your reality. If you aren't conscious of what you think about, nor have the understanding that you can shift your thoughts to think differently, then you automatically think the same or similar thoughts, and these are reinforced by attracting more comparable experiences. Most people don't see the connection amongst their beliefs, thoughts, and experiences. Most of us are not taught how or why these patterns re-occur.

How Is It You Believe What You Believe?

Growing up, we tended to believe what we were told, especially by our parents, but also by other authority figures such as teachers, coaches, and even friends. You have a lot of beliefs about what you can do, could do, should do. You also have beliefs that don't serve you. They are the ones where you think you can't, couldn't, or shouldn't. These are called limiting beliefs. We were all raised with them. Lots of them!

Our limiting beliefs often came from being managed and controlled in ways that made other people feel better. For example, when a child who is loud, enjoys big movement, and performs in an imaginary concert as if they are singing on stage, but is told to shut up, be quiet, stay still, or stop that noise, the impression the child gets is that he or she is wrong, bad, not enough, not worthy of pursuing their dream, or that they are unacceptable for having that desire, or acting in that way. The reason someone shut you up had nothing to do with you, but unfortunately, it adversely affected you. Your dad having a bad day at work and taking out his frustration on you when he got home was unfair, and interpreted by your young brain as there being something wrong with you or with what you were doing. But, there is *nothing* wrong with you, there never was, and when you can see this, you will begin again to start owning, and loving, that part of you that was squashed.

Limiting beliefs begin in childhood, and life would be so different if they stayed in childhood, but they don't. They follow us around for the rest of our lives and we believe them to be the truth until, like now, you learn new, enlightening information that opens up the possibility for you to see a new, different, more illuminating way. Can you imagine living in a way that is honoring you instead of suppressing you? A way that validates you, instead of oppressing you, making you feel unworthy? I can. because I've learned to live in this new, loving, compassionate, non-judgmental way. My mission here is to help you see this new way so that you can create the authentically happy, genuinely fulfilled life you desire.

It's Time for a Software Upgrade

Think of your brain as a new computer. This is how it was when you were born. Nice and clean with lots of space for downloads. As others downloaded information into your brain, there were positive downloads, but also negative downloads which we'll call viruses. Your little brain had no virus protection, no firewall, and no malware protection. Soon a trojan horse appears, spyware shows up, and mayhem ensues. Your hard drive ceases to function properly. The positive programs are slower to open; they aren't performing properly, they have glitches. Your best bet is to purchase a product and download the right protection for viruses, put up firewalls, upgrade your operating system, check for patches and check for updates. As you clean up your hard drive brain and put the proper protections in place, you get your positive programs, which are even better now, back up and running smoothly.

It's similar with your limiting beliefs. You can, quite literally, download into your brain (aka learn) new information and get better results. You can break apart your beliefs to see how you acquired them, by whom and why, and see which ones serve you and which ones don't. You can then learn to take the beliefs that don't work for you anymore, shift them, and experience a more empowering way to be with that belief.

For example, I used to complain about my dad all the time. I hated the way he treated me, so my words, body language, contorted face, curse words about him, and tone of voice all indicated the victim state I was in, for years, even decades, after leaving his house. I thought of myself as a loser, unworthy, and never quite felt whole. Although I wanted a happy life, I often spoke words that perpetuated the negative ways I felt. As I began to understand the difference between beliefs and truths, and became more consciously aware, my life became much easier to live in, and I became happier and more fulfilled. If you want to know more about how to shift in this way, I'm just a phone call away. I'm happy to share more about this with you.

Can Your Emotions Really Help You?

The answer is Yes! Your emotions, good or bad, give you so much information. Let me demonstrate through a story what happens when we pay attention to them and how life can be better when we do.

One day my friend Patty asked if I could drive her to the car dealership. The maintenance had been performed and the car was ready. While on our way there, a car started passing me on my left. In a highly animated way, arms waving about, and a look of deep upset, Patty yelled for me to speed up, to hurry, to not allow that car to get ahead of me. I was surprised at what I will call her high level of road rage even though I was driving. I remained calm and told her I didn't care if that car passed me. She continued with her high level of agitation. She insisted I comply, and when I didn't do what she wanted, she began screaming at me to let her out of my car. I refused to stop the car on this busy road not only because her request seemed unreasonable but we were almost to the dealership. Although I had no problem with a car passing us up, Patty was having very strong emotions about it. I attempted to reason with her again, but it didn't work.

When I did pull into the dealership, she angrily flung the door open, grabbed her purse, and with her face completely contorted, she slammed the door as hard as possible, and stormed away. She was so angry she couldn't speak. I was stunned. Patty and I have known each other for a long time. I've seen other odd behavior by her, but never anything like this. She had allowed the emotion she was having to get way out of hand. Patty felt completely justified in her anger toward me and could only see that I was wrong for not doing what she wanted me to do. Have you ever experienced someone else's anger because you didn't do what they wanted you to do?

Within a few months, we reconciled, and decided to go have lunch. She picked me up, and as usual, she was passing cars here and there. Not a big deal, until someone tried to pass her. Immediately that road rage kicked in. She battled for her life, and mine, to make sure that no one passed her. It was quite the scene, almost getting in a wreck, driving way faster than was safe, leaving me stunned, holding my breath, and white-knuckling it as it was happening. When it was over, and I had calmed down some, I mentioned how she was living a double standard, and her driving was dangerous.

I said, "I notice you pass cars regularly and seem to feel they should let you, but when someone tries to pass you, you change into a heightened state of road rage." And with that, she lost blew up at me, again. The short ending to this story is she kicked me out the car, we obviously didn't have lunch, and she decided we could no longer be friends.

Can you see my mouth ajar, eyes wide, and eyebrows lifting into my hairline?

This is a good example showing how our emotions rule us, how we just react when we are unaware of what is actually happening. Becoming conscious of, feeling, and naming our emotions allows us to use them to our advantage. Emotions are our guidance system. They let us know if we are heading toward what we want, or if we're headed toward what we don't want.

So let's look at what was happening with Patty. In childhood, Patty had been dismissed, demeaned, discounted, disregarded, and disrespected. Although she didn't make the connection, once she was behind the wheel of a 2,000 pound car, she found (unconsciously) an equalizer. Here she felt emboldened, brazen, seen, important, and in control. This showed up by staying ahead of, or getting ahead of, others. When this happened, she felt good about herself.

If, however, a car somehow got ahead of her she felt the discomfort of her childhood, and she felt bad about herself. When

I pointed it out to her it was too painful for her to acknowledge, and her anger showed up to protect her. Without feeling, acknowledging and processing her emotions, Patty had no choice but to *acquiesce to them*. Do you know this is true for all of us?

This story has a happy conclusion. After not speaking for several years, Patty and I reconnected. She shared with me that our conversation had a profound impact on her. She realized that her intense reactions while driving weren't really about the cars passing her; they stemmed from deeper issues linked to her past experiences. Understanding this, she has significantly changed her driving behavior. Now, she no longer experiences road rage and feels much happier, having made this personal breakthrough.

TAKEAWAYS:

- Integrity is important; your words, thoughts, and actions matter.
- Look for the clues your emotions are giving you. They reveal whether or not you're headed in the direction that's right for you.
- Core values are *core* for a reason.

Are you on a journey to embrace and honor your true self?

Dive into a world of self-exploration in our free, private, women-only Facebook group, the *Self-Discovery Lab*. Each month, we uncover and delve into new topics that celebrate and illuminate who you are—and who you're destined to be. Join us and connect with a supportive community of women just like you!
https://www.facebook.com/groups/selfdiscoverylab

6

If I Have to Do It, Why Doesn't He?

Breaking free of the emotional pain requires new information and skills.

Let's look at why it is important to learn how to live in a way that is *not* dependent on how others act, what they say or do, or how they behave. First, think about when you were growing up, you followed tons of rules, right? Certain ones are fairly common such as if you drop it, pick it up; if you turn it on, turn it off; if you spill it, wipe it up; if you open it, close it. You were expected to regularly attend to the mess you made. You were expected to be, or become, responsible for your actions. And, these messages were repeated throughout your life, and you've come to live by them.

But what happens when someone else makes the mess? They're supposed to clean it up, right? And what happens if the mess-maker is your dad? Isn't he supposed to clean up his mess? Of course he is because that's the rule he taught you. And so you wait…and wait…and that mess doesn't get cleaned up. The apology never comes. You end up waiting in a never-ending pattern of expecting your dad to fix his screw up. You hold on and hold on, hoping, wishing, and wanting for dad to fix the problem, but deep down inside, you know this will never happen. Dad's not changing, and it is so painful. I know that even as an adult you want him to fix it, I totally get that, because it's what I wanted too.

Your logical adult mind understands that it's unfair—he

made the mistake, and he should address it. Yet, part of you might hope he'll realize his error if you just wait a bit longer. Meanwhile, you might feel unworthy or unlovable, reminiscent of feelings from your childhood. If these feelings persist, it might be time to seek new information and start advocating for yourself. You deserve to be treated with respect and dignity.

Many rationalize that it has to be your parent that gives this loving, caring attention, but it's not true. This is the reason it's important to live in a way that is *not* dependent on how another acts. I have discovered that when you make the mistake of waiting for someone else to do what they should do, you end up making a lot of other types of mistakes, like dating jerk boyfriends, getting jobs that are victimizing, speaking stupidly to your friends, treating your kids unfairly, and none of that will result in living a better life. These are repeated patterns that create the same types of scenarios throughout your life. What might be possible if you decide to stop waiting for the other person to change or fix things?

Wanda's father was not emotionally available. She remembers desperately wanting a connection with her dad all during her childhood. After moving out on her own, she dated lots of men who were jerks, but luckily ended up marrying a man who did give her quite a bit of emotional connection. But for Wanda, it was never enough; she always craved more. She would often fight with her husband, Jerry, about this. He gave what he could and just couldn't understand why, no matter how much he gave, it was never enough.

In a coaching session, Wanda told me about their anniversary. Jerry had given her the present of a day at the spa, taken her out to eat dinner, and paid her a lot of attention. She admits it was wonderful, kind, and loving, and she appreciated all of it. The next day she had mentioned wanting to take a long soak later in the evening after she finished running some errands. She got home to find that Jerry had fixed supper for them and then sweetly, holding her hand, led her to the bathroom where he had set up candles, a glass for her wine, and had a special bubble bath treatment that he had purchased, all waiting for her. She said it was a delightful surprise.

She told me he ran the water to the perfect temperature, and that bubbles filled the tub. Before he left her to soak and relax, he lit all the candles, filled her glass with wine, and turned on some soft music. She said he gave her a kiss and then closed the door. "It was like a little piece of heaven," she said, and told me how much she had been enjoying all the attention.

When the water started getting too cool, she called out for Jerry to come back. She wanted him to warm the water for her, to continue to make her feel special. A few minutes later she called for him again, but he didn't come. She called him a final time, this time feeling angry. She wondered why he was doing this to her. He had been so sweet and now he was ignoring her.

Wanda told me that everything Jerry had done for her for the past two days now meant nothing. She shared how pissed she had gotten, and how justified she felt. Wanda got out of the tub, robed herself, and went looking for Jerry. She found him sitting at the kitchen table staring into space. She started in on him immediately, bombarding him with her anger. Why didn't he come when she called? Why was he ignoring her? Doesn't he know how upset that makes her? Why was he tricking her by being nice but taking it away?

I encouraged Wanda to reflect on her emotions and relationships. Through this process, she recognized how much Jerry had been supporting her emotionally and how happy this support made her feel. She also realized that her desire to feel special was not only directed towards Jerry but was a longing she had had for her father's affection, which she never received. Whenever Jerry momentarily stopped making her feel special, Wanda experienced a profound sense of worthlessness, echoing her childhood feelings. This reflection helped her understand that she was projecting her unresolved feelings about her father onto Jerry.

Wanda was attempting to heal her childhood wounds

through her relationship with Jerry, a common but ineffective strategy. This approach often leads to self-sabotage and can damage relationships. Jerry, who acted out of love, didn't deserve the anger directed at him, and his confusion was understandable. Through reflection, Wanda realized that her reactions were triggered by unresolved feelings from her childhood. She learned that although Jerry might trigger these feelings, he was not the root cause of her emotional pain.

At one point, I just had to ask, "Wanda, why didn't you just turn on the hot water and warm the water yourself?"

She said, "I swear, I never even thought of it. All I knew was that I just wanted Jerry to do it, and I got angry when he didn't."

The pain we inflict on ourselves by not being aware of our inner turmoil is profound. Life becomes much smoother when we take the time to observe our own behaviors. Often, we find that our expectations for others to intuitively understand our needs—even when we don't clearly understand them ourselves—are unrealistic. It's unfair to expect others to know what we need, just as it's unfair for them to expect us to anticipate their needs. Recognizing that your anger may be misdirected is vital for personal growth. When anger arises, take a moment to reflect: "What am I feeling? Where is this coming from? What need of mine is not being met?" Answering these questions can open up new possibilities. By pausing and considering what else might be possible, we allow our brains the space to reveal deeper insights and solutions.

Wanda shared one more observation about that night with me. When she saw Jerry in the kitchen, she had begun to unload on him by asking question after question about ignoring her and not coming when she called. She hadn't even given him the opportunity to get a word in edgewise. When she finally slowed down enough, he was able to tell her why he hadn't answered.

He had been looking out the kitchen window when he noticed a toddler, crying and walking barefoot down the middle of the street. He immediately ran outside to investigate. There had been an accident at the corner, and somehow the little one had slipped out of the car. As the police arrived, Jerry handed the child over to them. After being told he wasn't needed, Jerry returned to the house and had just sat down at the kitchen table when Wanda entered and started bombarding him with questions. Reflecting on it later, she realized she felt foolish for being so angry with Jerry, even though she felt justified at the time. Now, armed with new information and tools, she is grateful to have better ways to manage her anger. And needless to say, Jerry is much happier too.

Fire the Critic, Hire the Muse

I'll be honest, there was a time when I was very much like Wanda. I had to learn to stop making my problems everyone else's responsibility. I was desperate to stop the negative thoughts that constantly ran through my mind (self-sabotage). I also needed to stop being so critical of myself in my self-talk.

One day I made a decision. It was time for the critic's voice (dad's) to get out of my mind. I consciously decided to take back my life and live the way I felt was best for me (self-love). I decided to fire the critic and ask for my muse to move in. At the time, the best way for me to handle this was to write a letter. Here it is, unchanged:

Dear Critic,

You are fired! You have been the worst boss I've ever had. You have judged and criticized me more than anyone else in the entire world. You've been mean, ugly, rude, hateful, and relentless. You have used me as a scapegoat for your lack of power and lack of self-esteem…you are basically a bully. But guess what? I have hung in there through all of your nastiness, which makes me realize how strong I am.

I am still here, and I have summoned all my inner strength. I realize that while I have allowed you to be in charge, this is not your mind. It is my mind. And so, in the name of all that is good, hopeful, kind, and loving inside of me, I fire you and bid you farewell.

I have hired a new boss and she is wonderful. She is playful, she appreciates me, loves me, is adventurous, exciting, fun, and a bit daring. I have called in my muse for she is who I shall be looking to from now on. Your time in my head, Critical Dad voice, is over—good-bye and good riddance.

Hello, my muse. Me and my precious inner child welcome you. Together we have taken over the controls. Let the wild, new ride begin.

And so, my journey toward self-mastery began, and it's an experience I wouldn't trade for the world. While it has had its easy moments and its challenges, it has undoubtedly been the most rewarding endeavor of my life. I made this decision because, like you, I realized I have the power to change. I want you to recognize that you also hold the power to continuously seek greater happiness in your life. It starts with small steps that gradually grow. Yes, it requires practice, but what could be more important than living your best, most fulfilled life?

Drawing a Line in the Sand Is a Beautiful Thing

About twenty-five years ago, I discovered Friedensreich Hundertwasser, the incredible Austrian visionary artist and spiritual ecologist. He hated the straight line and went to great depths to discredit it, even calling it godless and the downfall of humanity. His passion for attempting to get people to understand how he felt was immense. Consider his observation: "The line I trace with my feet walking to the museum is more important and more beautiful than the lines I find there hung up on the walls."

In a sense, he was not only tracing the beauty of the line with his feet, he was drawing a line in the sand. He stood up for what he believed. He was not willing to compromise what he knew to be true for him.

Drawing a line in the sand is a beautiful thing. It makes the statement to others that you know what you want and are no longer willing to accept what has been. Drawing your line may be a surprise to a lot of people, but it is your line and you have every right to draw it. It is your statement of what you will accept and what you won't. It is telling people—even though they may not understand it— that you love yourself enough to make a difference in your own life. It is you showing self-love for you. It is a powerful feeling to care for yourself in a way that no one else possibly can.

Look to yourself for appreciation and validation as you draw this line. You really don't need anyone else's permission if the reasons you are making the changes are for your own self-betterment. I can promise you that this line is going to make certain people upset, and if you are more worried about how they feel and what they think, you are likely to allow them to erase your line, make your line shorter, or possibly you may not make one at all. Know that you may stand alone, at least for a while. Know it may be a bit lonely, but you will survive. In fact, drawing the line and holding steady will allow you to thrive. If you want to change your life, sometimes you must make hard decisions. It's just the way it is. But what I know is that if you put your mind to it, you can do this. If you can't, I'm here.

Continue to experience the deep self-knowing you are learning about. All this information you are learning is helping you become aware of what's going on inside of you. Most people never learn this, and that's why their lives don't change. If you want change in your life, you must know what you want it to look like; in other words, you create it. You must make decisions and create boundaries, and sometimes it's important to create strong boundaries.

I've personally discovered who I am, and I will tell you that I now choose not to change my shape to fit into other people's puzzles. I have my own shape and when I don't fit, I realize that I just don't belong in that puzzle. I've learned this, and you are learning it too. How much happier can life be when you are so clear of your puzzle shape that you love every curve of it, and you're not adversely affected that you don't fit all puzzles everywhere, all the time?

Fear Can Be Your Friend

Sometimes making changes feels scary. This is completely normal. That's right, it is normal to feel fear and discomfort when you are drawing that line because, like I said, there are certain people who aren't going to be happy about it. But this is where fear can be your friend.

You are feeling fear because your body knows you are getting ready to do something bold. Not a lot of people have the courage to do what you want to do, but that makes you an extraordinary person. It makes you someone who is willing to be an advocate for yourself. It says you are willing to do for your happiness what others won't—or can't—do for theirs. Do you realize how many people are willing to live miserable their entire lives because they're afraid to upset someone else?

Check the feeling you are having. Is it really fear, or could it possibly be excitement? Fear and excitement have similar vibrations. Whichever the feeling, feel it, experience it, embrace the emotion, draw that line. Lean into self-love and let the self-sabotage go.

Sometimes You Just Have to Walk Out

When my son was just over a year old, we moved about 400 miles away from my hometown. Whenever we returned for visits, we stayed with my parents. On one visit, when my son was about two and a half, I was in the kitchen talking with my mom when I heard my father yell at my son in the same harsh tone he had always used with me. But this time, things were different. I was no longer just his daughter; I was a mother now.

I don't recall jumping up or flying through the house, but all of a sudden, I was at the bathroom door where the yelling was happening. I knew my dad had an anger problem, and I did not want my child to be the brunt of that bullshit. I pushed my way past my dad to get in between him and my son. Shielding my son, I stood facing my father in a posture that was like a mama bear protecting her cub. I'm not sure where it came from, but I drew upon a surge of emotional strength I didn't know I had.

When I asked why he was yelling at my child like that, my dad's reply was because my son had "wasted" toilet paper by unrolling some of it on the floor. I was pissed but my speech was calm. I said, "He's two and a half. He doesn't understand what he's doing. Maybe there is a better way to handle this than by using that tone." As usual, my father's response was hostile and confrontational indicating he was the boss and the one who makes the decisions.

He growled at me, eyes narrowed, "If he does that shit again, I'm gonna beat his ass."

For a second, I froze. I knew he would do it, and I felt lost and didn't know what to do. My body trembled, my hands were shaking, I felt the tears coming. Staying at his house was no longer an option. We had to leave, but why did I feel as if I was the one doing something wrong? I was being forced into a situation of choosing between keeping all the secrets, keeping the status quo, allowing this man to dominate again, or deciding to do something different. Even in all of my fear and discomfort, I chose to do something different.

I called a family member and asked if we could stay at their house. We could. I packed up all our stuff and started loading it into the car. My dad tried a number of ways to stop me including telling me how stupid I was acting, how silly I was to be leaving, and standing in the way of us getting out of the door. Somehow I got myself and my son in the car and drove off.

It turned out to be a powerful moment for me. I realized

that I needed to do the right thing for me and my son regardless of how it made my dad feel. When I look back, I'm not sure it phased my dad at all. I know it made my mom sad, but this was one of those times where it was important to make smart decisions and put healthy boundaries in place, even if it meant someone being uncomfortable about the change. This was me doing the right thing for the right people at the right time. This shift began a new habit for me.

Creating new habits is easier when you understand how the brain works. Think of the olden days when people used a horse and buggy. They would go down the same path over and over, and soon the earth moved to the sides and created ruts. The ruts were desirable if you wanted to go the same way; they even helped guide the oxen because it helped keep the wheels in the deeper parts of the path. But if you wanted to turn off that path, getting the wheels out of the rut and over the bank was difficult. Doable, yes, but it took effort.

The same holds true in our brains. We say, think, and act the same way over and over. These are habits even if they don't feel that way. In essence, we wear ruts into our brain (create neuropathways), and it's difficult when we want to change to a different path. It is, however, necessary if we desire to create change. Creating new thoughts and then repeating those new thoughts is akin to going down the new path over and over. The repetition establishes new neuropathways, and they are the ones *you* choose, not those chosen by others.

Loving from Afar Is Still Loving

If you've tried a variety of approaches and nothing has worked, you may find it necessary to remove your dad (or the toxic person) from your life, at least for a little while, or possibly forever if that's what you decide. Choosing to remove yourself from participating with a toxic person does not mean you don't love them anymore, nor does it mean you are the bad guy. It just means you need time on your own to wear some of those new neuro pathways so that you can think more for yourself without the influence of others.

I remember when I made the conscious decision to remove myself from being around my dad. It meant removing myself from spending time with other family members too, at least for a while. Was it hard? Yes. Was it worth it? Definitely. Pulling away is taking a stand. It is making a statement ... and ... if you are going to do it, make sure you mean it. Meaning, don't promise something if you're not going to carry through with it. For example, promising you'll never go to your dad's house again as a threat and then showing up the next month is not an example of taking a stand. Promising that you will leave if he insults you (or whatever your situation is) and then you leave when he insults you, is taking a stand. But again, make sure you carry through with whatever you say you are going to do or you will not be taken seriously.

I am neither a therapist nor a law enforcement officer, and I'm not prescribing any specific actions. However, if you ever feel physically threatened or believe you might benefit from therapy, I strongly encourage you to reach out to the appropriate professionals or authorities who are equipped to help in your situation. Do not hesitate to seek support you need.

TAKEAWAYS

- Make a habit of observing your behaviors, and remember that the better you love and care for yourself, the better you can love and care for others.
- Care and love aren't what you wait to receive from someone else; care and love are *waiting for you to **give these to yourself***. If you also get care and love from others, all the better.

7
Be Unstoppable For Yourself

Do what you can with what you've got, from where you are ... and keep moving forward.

A client of mine, Valerie, had horrible experiences with her dad. There was much physical and emotional abuse in the house she grew up in. Seeing a ping-pong paddle or plastic tie straps sent waves of fear through her body. The adult Valerie understands she will not be punished like that anymore, but the child inside still remembers. It has been incredibly difficult for Valerie to be in a mature relationship, especially with men, for fear they will hurt her, either physically or emotionally.

Although Valerie did date occasionally, the relationship could only go so far. She would get to a certain point and start to push back. She would find everything wrong with the man she was dating and would even pick fights. She was sabotaging the relationship hoping the boyfriend would break up with her. It seemed easier that way.

One man, however, did end up getting through her emotional roadblocks, and she enjoyed being with him. At some point, he asked her to marry him. She cared for him, loved him in the way that she was able, and wanted to marry, but she wouldn't. She felt her childhood trauma and inner turmoil was so deep that she could not put him through being in a relationship with someone who was so emotionally immature and unavailable. She felt breaking up with him was the right and fair thing to do. He protested. She insisted, and they did break up, but she has suffered from her decision ever since.

This was yet one more excruciating event in her life, and she blames almost every bad thing on the abuse she received from her father. Finally, at forty-three years old, Valerie decided she'd had enough of the fear, internal turmoil, and what felt like open sores that never healed, and she wanted the pain to stop. Valerie contacted me and decided to work with me.

While sharing her story, tears ran down her cheeks. Valerie had spent years internalizing her father's harsh words, believing she was useless and unworthy. Despite her success in her career, she couldn't shake the feeling of never being enough. Lost and confused, she didn't know what steps to take or where she ultimately wanted to end up, but she was certain of one thing: she no longer wanted to remain in this painful state. As we worked together, she soon began to feel she was stepping out of a bad dream. Step-by-step she discovered the real Valerie behind the façade. As this false shell imposed by others began to fade away, as she discovered more about her authentic self.

Valerie told me, "I feel lighter and calmer, like I had been desperately searching for something and now I've found it. I am not who he said I was. I am me, a whole and authentic person." Years of guilt, sadness, victimization, familial drama, and struggle lifted. And now that she has surfaced into her new awareness of herself and her new way of living, she feels unstoppable.

Writing Them Down

How important is it to write down your goals and dreams? A Harvard study showed that of all the graduates from Harvard, only the 3 percent that had *written goals* succeeded to the level they set for themselves; the other 97 percent did not. Writing down your goals is an important component to success. (Keep in mind to use your definition of success.)

Why are most people resistant to writing down their goals? Maybe it's a fear of failure, or maybe it's a fear of success. Either way, it's fear. As I've stated several times, when you don't know your real, true, authentic self it is difficult to know what you want because you are worried about what others might think of your choices. When you do know yourself deeply, creating goals is not only easy, it's fun, exciting, and desirable, because you are choosing what you want regardless if others agree with your decisions or not. Remember, this is about your life and what you want, not about others.

I hear people challenging me already, "....but I have a partner, I have kids. I can't just do what I want." You're right. I'm not asking you to abandon your responsibilities, but I am asking you to observe what they are and if you are choosing them, or if they are being chosen for you, or if you are doing them because you think you have to. You have choices. Look at your life, see what's upsetting, observe how you feel when you are performing certain tasks, and see what other possibilities there are. Who knows? Maybe you're better at creative problem solving that you thought.

Back to goals. It's exciting to write down goals and dreams you want to pursue. Once they are written, read them aloud to yourself, a lot. A shift will occur where your brain begins to accept this new information. When you know where you want to end up, your motivations and actions will consistently lead you in that direction. I promise you the brain will begin to accept your new desires and start responding differently. I'll explain the science behind it further in this chapter.

For now, use the Personal Profile Tool and record where you would like to see yourself in ten years, five years, and in one year. Yep, start with the ten-year goal first, and you can record material items if you like, but definitely record the nonphysical ones, like how calm you want your life to be, your happiness level, the amount of joy you want to have, and who you'd like to have in your life. Imagine them, create them. Decide where you want to go. How big can you dream?

Next, write down at least one goal that you would like to accomplish in the next two to three months. You may even want to break that down into smaller, more manageable steps. Small steps, even micro-steps, get you where you want to go. When I backpacked the 500-miles across Spain, I made it to the end of my journey by taking one step at a time. Step-by-step, large or small, is the only way *anyone* ever gets anything done.

I'm excited we're at the part where you are making these decisions and creating your goals. I love that you are taking responsibility for the life you want to have. This is how you bring desired outcomes into your life.

Do What You Can...

Do what you can, from where you are, with what you've got, and keep moving forward. With that in mind, how might your life be different if you started taking full responsibility for the direction you wanted to go in? What do you think would happen if you stopped waiting for someone else to fix your pain, to change, to die or leave, or alter something? How much happier would you be if you stopped blaming, shaming, or complaining about what was happening in your life?

Think of it this way: You are an adult and you are in charge of yourself. If you didn't like the way things were in the house you grew up in, you have the *right* to do things differently. It is a decision that *only you* should make. Be unstoppable for yourself.

This is the power of taking control of your life. Set your compass, or GPS, and go toward what you desire. Time is going to pass anyway. We can't stop time. However, what we can do is decide how we want to spend our time. And when you *decide with conviction*, something amazing happens; it's like the universe hears you and begins to conspire in your favor.

The Importance of Intentions

Having goals is awesome. And to make them even better, let's add in intentions. Goals without having intentions is like taking a bubble bath in cold water with no bubbles. The water gets the job done, but it's not really any fun. Intentions are the warmth (water) and playfulness (bubbles) you get to enjoy along the way. Intentions are you giving yourself permission to be happier, more successful, and more abundant on many levels *while you are headed* toward the goals you set.

If you are going to travel the distance, why not enjoy the trip? Can you imagine taking a two-day road trip and being frustrated the whole time until you get to your destination? Could you imagine not enjoying a phone conversation or listening to a podcast, not singing a song or listening to music, not eating or enjoying food while traveling? And then, after you reach your destination, only then can you decide you can enjoy yourself? That would be crazy ... and miserable.

For each step you take toward your goal, why can't you have the most enjoyment possible in each moment? Sure, some steps will have little enjoyment, but then there will be steps where lots of enjoyment can be had. Why ignore those? It's up to you to recognize all the little moments where enjoyment can be had, and it's up to you to stop expecting anyone else to create enjoyment for you.

Did I make that sound too hard? It's not really. Did you know that you set intentions all the time? You do. But I want you to make sure that you are creating intentions from the conscious part of your brain, and not from the unconscious part. Let's first take a look at what creating unconsciously looks like.

Unconsciously Created Intentions ...
- Are not well thought out
- Are often a reaction to something someone did (possibly retaliation)
- Sometimes are made because of others in your family
- Sometimes are made because that's the way it's always been

- Can direct you by default (via automatic behavior, old patterns, habits, etc.)

With Consciously Created Intentions ...

- You have a clear sense of direction
- You can be authentically true to you
- Your confidence increases
- You pay attention to your inner feelings, wants, and needs
- Self-regulation and clarity are abundant
- Your wisdom grows
- You invest in yourself
- You shape, shift, and positively alter your life

Don't think it must be perfect before you start. Intentions, like goals, come in many shapes and sizes, and they come in all levels and degrees of difficulty and length of time. Some intentions might be to smile more, to stop imitating others, to notice how you are genuinely feeling, to enjoy the moment, to be consciously aware of your thoughts, or maybe to find more purpose in your life.

Some are for the duration of a goal, and some are lifelong and there is no end, such as, "Every day, for the rest of my life, I want to see beauty in the world." The difference is that goals are more *out there somewhere,* and intentions allow us to experience what's going on *in here, inside ourselves.*

I have an intention I use every day: "I want to live in a world where love wins, where the love of power is overshadowed by the power of love." And because of this intention, everything I think, say, and do (including writing this book), the goals I create, the dreams and desires I have are all in alignment with this intention. Living a happy, fulfilled, successful life takes time, desire, focus, course corrections, and dedication, but what's the alternative? Life is going to happen, time is going to pass. Why not make goals and intentions for the life *you* want?

The Science: Shift Happens

Here's the science I mentioned earlier: the Reticular Activating System (RAS). Nestled in the lower part of your brain, this small but mighty section is tasked with filtering the vast amounts of information bombarding your sensory organs.

The Reticular Activating System is a small, intensely woven bundle of nerves that reads all the stimuli your senses (except smell) experience every second of every day, awake or sleeping. It serves as the gatekeeper to your conscious mind. This system selects the most crucial data for your conscious awareness while discarding the rest. For instance, consider a sleeping mother who awakens at her newborn's faint cry, demonstrating the RAS's ability to prioritize essential signals.

Why do we require this gatekeeper? Because, at any given time, we are bombarded with up to two million data bits per second (bps), yet the RAS only allows approximately 100 bps through. This significant contrast highlights the overwhelming amount of sensory input our brains receive. Therefore, the RAS plays a vital role in determining which information merits our attention and which can be ignored.

How does the Reticular Activating System discern what's important? Surprisingly, it relies on your focus. If you're concentrating on something—anything—the RAS interprets it as significant because you're giving it attention.

Let's do a real-time experiment:

Take about five seconds and look around counting everything red that you see. Really do this, as in stop reading, look around and count, it's important. Got your number? Now, without looking, tell me how many blue objects you saw. I know I said red and now I'm asking you about blue. If your brain is focused on red things, you'll see red shirts, red pencils, and a red book cover. Your brain won't pay attention to the blue chair, blue shoes, and blue file folder. If we focus on red objects, we see lots of them, and even though the blue things are there, we don't see them, because we aren't focused on them.

So what do you think would happen if you looked for blue things? Try it out. Take about five seconds and look around. Count everything blue that you see. Got your number? Now tell me how many yellow objects you saw.

Let's say red represents negativity, blue represents positivity, and yellow represents opportunity. All around us, every day, are red (negativity), blue (positivity), and yellow (opportunity). What you focus on is what the RAS determines is important, which are allowed through the gatekeeper into the conscious mind, or you wouldn't be focused on it. It does not know positive, negative, or opportunity, it only knows if you're giving your attention to it (aka focused on it), then it is important and you will experience more of that.

This is the science that governs our lives. When you're focused on your new goals and intentions (blue as positivity and yellow as opportunity), that signals the RAS to determine them as important. As they begin to seep into your consciousness more and more, you will begin to see, feel, and experience more of what you want because that is what you are focusing on more. But be warned, the opposite is also true. The more you focus on what you don't want (red things aka negativity), the more you will see that too. It's a little tricky, but you'll understand this more as you practice and pay attention to it.

Let me share about a client who was challenged with the relationship she had with her father. It's an excellent example of how the Reticular Activating System works by using practice, focus, and dedication. This helped her heal certain aspects of her relationship with her father:

Sarah often felt distant from her father, John. Despite his presence in her life, Sarah sensed a barrier between them, stemming from unresolved issues and unspoken emotions.

Determined to mend their relationship, Sarah learned about the Reticular Activating System (RAS) and its role in filtering information. She realized that her focus on past grievances and misunderstandings might be reinforcing negative perceptions of her father.

Sarah decided to shift her attention. Instead of dwelling on past conflicts, she started actively seeking positive interactions with her father. She made a conscious effort to notice and appreciate his efforts, however small, to connect with her.

As Sarah began to focus on the moments of warmth and understanding between them, she noticed a gradual shift in their relationship. John responded positively to her newfound openness and willingness to engage with him.

With time, Sarah and her father developed a stronger bond built on mutual respect and understanding. By using the power of her RAS to prioritize the positive aspects, she was able to heal the wounds of the past and forge a healthier relationship with her father.

Living the principles of deep inner self-knowing, and using loving, compassionate, non-judgmental ways of being brings greater awareness in your life. The beautiful part is it gets easier with time and practice.

TAKEAWAYS

- Write down your goals and intentions and let everything you think, say, and do move you toward your end result.
- Use your RAS to notice the events you desire; remember, this little gatekeeper allows into your conscious mind what you *focus on*. Focus more on blue things (positive) and yellow things (opportunities).

8
No More Locked Rooms

The locked room is now unlocked forever.

I hope you realize that nothing you did as a child is your fault. You did *nothing* wrong to start this craziness. There is no way, as a child, you could have been responsible for what happened or know what to do or how to get people to act differently. You were in survival mode. Survival. Getting through one day and to the next day without additional repercussions – that was your goal.

What you can do now, though, is observe what happens and why and use these tools to do something about living in a different way. Just because things were done a particular way in the house you grew up in, doesn't mean you need to continue to do them, especially if they feel uncomfortable or wrong. Let's look at some information that is fairly new, wasn't taught in school, our parents probably weren't aware of, and you may not be either, until now.

We are adults, but the emotional upset created during childhood still permeates our lives. We were raised by adult children who were raised by adult children who were raised by adult children, who were…you get the picture. Until recently there was not enough accessible data to help the average person figure out how to get unstuck. Basically, humans have been stuck in the muck for generation after generation. That is beginning to change, and I'd venture to guess that you are reading this book because something inside of you agrees with wanting to break the mold. I know this is true for me. I wanted things to change.

My father showed me all the ways I did *not* want to be. For example, when I was growing up, no matter what I did, no matter how well I might have performed, his attitude was that I could have always done better and that I was not worthy of his acknowledgment or praise - ever. When asked why he never gave me a compliment (again not ever), his response was that he didn't want me to get "a swell-head." If I did poorly, I was berated. If I did well, I could have done better. I was treated crappy and never knew why.

My father believed strongly in the traditional male/female roles. In his eyes, a female's purpose in life is to cook, clean, and generally take care of the man's needs. When I wanted to go to college, his response was, "You're a girl and just going to get married and have babies. Why would I waste my money on you?" When my mom convinced him to rent a piano for me, when I was 9 years old, which I didn't even know about, he bent over me, one hand on his hip, the other waving menacingly over me, screaming down at me, "I don't even know why I'm wasting my money on you. You'll never amount to anything!" There's more, but you get the picture.

As I look back over my life, I think I disagreed with him on just about everything, and as you can imagine it just pissed him off. He wanted to be dominant, and he wanted me to be subservient. Period. And, even after moving out of his house, my dad wanted to continue to control my life, to dominate me and decide for me how I was going to live. Does any of this feel familiar to you? This is what I've come to understand:

It's not my fault my life was this way, but it sure did affect me negatively. I have learned that what happened in my childhood may not have been my fault, but as an adult it is my *responsibility* to make sure that I treat myself with dignity and respect and discover all I need to in order to live a life that makes me happy, feel worthy, and fulfilled. And I'm happy to report that I've reached this beautiful place, and I want nothing more than for you to reach it too.

Triggering Your Triggers

I remember the time when my friend Jeremy told me he was going to send me something in the mail. We talked about him taking the package to the post office and that I would get it a few days later. I excitedly waited for the package, looking out for it every day. A couple of days after the package should have arrived, I called him to say that I had not yet gotten it. What happened next turned out to be an incredible moment of becoming aware of my patterns and habits. This allowed me to decide if I wanted to keep moving in the same direction or if I wanted to shift slightly to begin practicing a new way of being.

"Hey, I've been looking for that package you told me you were sending, but I haven't gotten it yet. It's been over a week and I feel like it should have gotten here by now."

"Oh, wow, I forgot to tell you, but I wasn't able to get to the post office when I thought I would, and I just mailed it two days ago," he said.

For a moment I couldn't speak. I could feel an upsetting emotion inside of me start to boil. He told me he was going to mail it that previous Friday and here we were talking almost ten days later and I'm finding out he only mailed it a couple days ago. I'm not sure which emotion was strongest (anger, disrespect, betrayal, deceit). I responded to him in a derogatory and accusatory tone. In my mind he was wrong and I was right. I felt justified being angry because he told me he was going to mail the package on a certain day, but he hadn't.

On top of that, he didn't reveal this information to me. Instead, I found out on my own. I had been on the lookout every day for the package to show up, checking to see if there was a box on my porch. How dare he not let me know. I can tell you I felt victimized by him and, therefore, quite justified in my feelings of speaking rudely to him.

He tried to calm me down so he could explain. He also

mentioned being shocked at my tone. I tried to hold myself together and act maturely, but I couldn't shake the upset. He tried again, and in different ways, to try to help me understand what had happened, but I found I got more and more angry every time he would not take the blame. How could he do this to me? I thought he was my friend, and friends don't do that to each other. I was hurt, but what showed was anger. I didn't realize how harsh I was coming across.

The contention became so heated that he said, "Debbie, if you don't change how you're talking to me, I'm hanging up." That shocked me. He screwed up, but I have to change the way I'm speaking? And yet something inside of me knew he was serious, and his friendship meant so much to me that I began to force myself to calm down. It was hard to do, but finally I did.

As was typical for us, we began to talk about what happened. We worked hard to just observe and not judge. It wasn't about whether or not he mailed the package or why he did or didn't say anything. It was about my go-to negative energy of anger and blaming when something goes awry. It was about observing everything, especially my reaction to what had happened.

As we discussed and picked this situation apart and began to dig into what was really going on with me, I began to see that so much of the emotional abuse I had sustained in childhood stayed with me all these years and spilled over into my friendships, work, and pretty much every aspect of my life. Although I had done the work to let go of the anger toward my dad, I had not understood how that same anger was infiltrating other aspects of my life, and how often I felt like a victim.

I am so thankful to have Jeremy in my life. He stayed on the phone with me for five hours that night while I cried and while we worked through it trying to help me figure out what was underneath all the anger. We observed when life doesn't quite go my way, I immediately start to shame, blame, or complain. We observed when something happens I immediately get triggered from events that happened in the past, even though I didn't realize

I was doing that. We observed that as I speak loudly and rudely, I falsely feel a sense of power but I'm really doing it because I feel powerless. And the biggest observation was the recognition of violated core values.

As all of this came into my conscious awareness, it was as if a fog was lifted, like the lights were turned on. I could finally see what I had not been able to see before. Relief flooded my body. I relaxed. Suddenly, life made some sense. He had triggered a trigger, but he was *not the cause* of the trigger. So many times I had reacted in similar ways to others, and not known why. Now, I knew. It has been such a relief to learn this. The amazing part is how much I've changed because of knowing this. I have no need to respond that way anymore, and my life is much happier because of it.

Jumping on the Drama Triangle

Observing those feelings and recognizing my core values made me realize that I have the need for honesty, integrity, and respect, and when I didn't get it, a certain anger would come over me. There may be no ill intent, like with the reason that Jeremy couldn't mail the package on the day he thought he was going to, however, in my mind, every negative feeling I was feeling was his fault, and I was blaming him.

I knew this is not acceptable, but that evening I had to work hard to try and understand this new concept of "every feeling I feel is my responsibility." I've learned that I can't stop a feeling from coming into my mind, but I can decide how long I am going to allow it to affect my life. I've learned that the minute I get angry, I can immediately ask myself which of my needs are being violated or unmet, and I can calm down because I am able to associate them with childhood trauma and remind myself that the person in front of me is not the person who created the deep wound, and they do not deserve the brunt of my anger from childhood upsets.

In my search for answers, some really important information came my way. I learned about the drama triangle,

I JUST WANT TO BE HAPPY!

which has three roles: persecutor, rescuer, and victim. The drama triangle reveals how often we, as humans, males and females alike, fall into the role of victim. We move from role to role depending on the situation, often starting in one particular role most of the time, but then we move in or out of the roles just by the situation shifting. Bare with me, and I'll explain.

Regardless of where we start, we end up finding ourselves in a place where we feel powerless, upset, and frustrated—basically a victim. I want to help you understand why that is and what to do about it.

The illustration shows the abbreviated versions of the victim roles created by Jack Russell and Glenda Otto of the Center for Self-Sustaining Leadership. With permission granted, Jack and Glenda combined and interpreted the work of Stephen Karpman, MD, and Lynne Forrest's books on the drama triangle (see References).

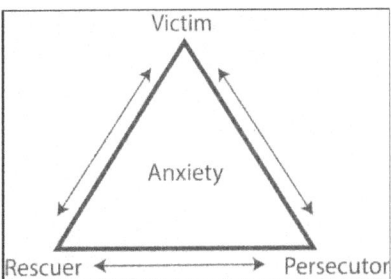

I find it interesting how many people can share who these three voices remind them of. Where do you step on the triangle? Who else can you recognize?

PERSECUTOR_(Voice of tyrant-bully-critical parent; culture of dominance and violence we accept as "the way it is."):_ I have power over you. I'm right. You're wrong. I have the right to judge, dismiss, and punish. I insist (I know) that my way of seeing things is right. You should change. You should do it my way. I don't have to change. I'm bigger (smarter) than you. I know what's best. I set the standards and the rules. If I scare you, tough. It's your problem.

I take charge. I'm in control. Results and bottom line (mine) are what count. I hide my fear by being a bully. I'm a coward. I often hurt people without knowing it. I can appear to be cruel. I count on you to not stand up to me. If you do, I'll attack, blame, deny, and justify that I'm right.

NUTSHELL: I'm right. You're wrong. You should do as I say. If you don't, I'll put you down, hurt you, or punish you.

RESCUER *(Voice of codependent caretaker who means to do well for others but doesn't know how to care for or stand up for themselves)*: You need my help. Other people have power over me. I'll take care of you. I'll make things right for you. I have the answers. I can fix things. I do for you what you could do for yourself. I always care for others. I only wish someone would care for me. I act as though I have no needs of my own. Maybe if I help you, I'll feel worthwhile myself and feel like I have some power. I often think I'm not enough as I am. I'm a good person. I'm not mean…but I often complain, act like a martyr, vent, and talk behind your back. I can't afford to be afraid…so I can't see how fearful and defensive I am. I won't take responsibility for the way I think, feel, and act. When the chips are down, I may try to control and manipulate… but I'm there for you.

NUTSHELL: I'll help you, help you, help you. Wait a minute, how do I stand up for myself? Hope someone will save me.

VICTIM *(Voice of victim; culture of subjection, compliance, and violence we accept as "the way it is.")*: I have no power. You run the show. I have little if any choice. I know you'll attack me, put me down, and deprive me of what I need or want if I speak up. I comply out of fear for our relationship, my job, my support. My future is in your hands. You won't listen anyway. I make excuses for the way you treat me. This isn't fair. It shouldn't be this way. I can't have what I want, so why ask? I can't think of how to say what I want to say. I'm trapped. I can't stand up for myself. I don't trust you. You'll make me out to be a fool. My thoughts and feelings circle around fear, pain, frustration, anger (mixed with guilt and shame). I often feel hopeless and helpless. I blame you (everyone) when things don't go my way. I keep hoping someone will save me. I deny and try to hide all of this from myself and from you...while I put up a good front.

NUTSHELL: This isn't right. It shouldn't be this way. You have the power. I have none. I'm alone. I'm trapped.

Who did you recognize? What about yourself, did you see your voice in any of this? If so, I invite you to notice how you may display these roles. You may be able to see yourself in all three roles depending on the situation, because we do bounce around, but we usually have one of the roles as the primary one. Please add your primary role to the Personal Profile Tool and observe the sabotaging ways it affects your life. As a gentle reminder, you can only change what you can consciously identify.

I know a lot of this is painful information. Humans don't like to feel pain or discomfort of any kind, especially our own emotional pain. But if you don't look at it, if you don't examine how it is affecting you, your family, your relationships, and your work, you will continue to live in a state of constant avoidance. Avoidance keeps you in the role of victim. And, unfortunately, avoiding the pain does not make the pain go away. Just the opposite happens. The more the pain shows up, the louder and more painful it becomes, and the more you shove it down, push it away, or pretend it doesn't exist, the more persistent it becomes (remember the RAS). Dealing with the pain is the only way to get it to go away, even if that means you go through some short-term emotional discomfort.

A Way to Sit with the Pain

I was watching a movie that brought up all kinds of emotions for me. I wasn't crying, but I could feel tremendous sadness and upset. The way the father in the movie treated his son felt so familiar to how I was raised that my heart just went out to this boy.

I winced when the father said, "What the hell is wrong

wit' you, boy?" and "Can't you do anything right?" I caught my breath when the father smacked the boy up the backside of his head and said, "Why do you have to screw up everything?" I knew that sensation all too well. I sensed the child-me inside growing sadder. My head dropped down, the corners of my mouth drooped, and my eyes cast down to the floor. I paused the movie and just sat with this pain.

Within a few seconds my eyes were closed as I remembered upsetting scenarios from my own life. My sadness grew, the tears were imminent. I felt smaller, younger, and powerless. Why had my dad treated me this way? What did I ever do? Why didn't my dad seem to love me?

As that thought came in my mind, another thought, from somewhere else said, "He did love you in his weird way. How did he love you? Tell me."

For a moment I wanted to figure out where that thought came from, but I was pulled back to the place of answering the question. My thoughts raced. Surely my dad loved me. In some weird, twisted, immature, dysfunctional way, he had to ... he just had to. I began to think about anything that could remind me of something he did that was proof to me that he loved me, and I found some. I also began to think about the words I had yearned him to say to me during my life.

I could picture him standing in the kitchen doorway. There was something different about his demeanor. Although he stood there looking like I had seen him dressed so many times, with the button up, short-sleeve, blue and red plaid shirt tucked into those polyester royal blue slacks, the thick-soled black tie-up shoes, and that horrible threatening black belt, he no longer had the tense posture of a bully. Instead of hands on hips, a denigrating look on his face, nose wrinkled back in disgust, towering over me, in my vision, he had the posture of a remorseful energy. His shoulders hung down, his body less tense, arms by his side. His head and eyes pointed toward the floor. He had a strange, sad look on his face and his brow appeared apologetic, maybe even sorrowful. I was glad he looked this way. I had wanted to see him look this way many times.

As if I knew what to do, I asked him to tell me words I had yearned to hear. He didn't seem capable, so I said the words and asked for his acknowledgment of them. I said things like, "I was special and wonderful," and watched him nod. I then spoke of the times when he had treated me crappy and had him acknowledge that. I had him acknowledge to me that he had respect for me, that he was impressed with what I had accomplished, and that he even appreciated my strength and resolve. In my vision, I had him nod in agreement that I was smart and that at times I had intimidated him. I expressed that I knew he had love for me, even though he never told me, and watched as he again nodded in agreement. I said all the words for him that I had always wanted him to say to me when he was alive, and I watched in my mind's eye as he nodded and acknowledged all of them.

And then, when I was done, and just sitting, eyes still closed, being in the moment, the most surprising words came out of *his* mouth, ones that surprised me.

He, or his spirit, or my vision of him, said, "I gave you everything I had; I just had so little to give." And with that my mind's eye immediately saw his parents, and I saw the incredibly screwed up way that they were and how he was treated as a child, and I understood how the little boy inside of him had been screaming his whole life in emotional heartache and pain and crying out for help. I believe it was the first time I had ever seen the vulnerability of this person I had called Dad.

I cried and sobbed, loud and hard, and I have no idea for how long. Finally, I went in the bathroom and cleaned the snot and tears from my face. As I walked back into the living room, I had the sudden realization that I had no more emotionally charged energy toward him, no more negativity, animosity, hate, no more anything really. The only emotion I had for him was sorrow. It was a strange sensation to have over fifty-seven years of hatred dissipate in one afternoon. But it did happen this way, and it has stayed gone.

Being able to resolve my anger toward him has helped a lot, but there was still the residual damage inside of me I had to deal with. Wanting to live my life in a way that is healthy, happy, productive, and heart-centered, I knew I had more work to do, but I looked forward to it. I knew it would be worth it.

Sitting with this pain and allowing it to surface, seeing it, feeling it, acknowledging the fullness of it, and then the release of it is a bit like being locked in a room and trying to get out. No windows, one door, no key. Clues available to find the key but disappointment at every turn. And then, finally, the key is found, the door is unlocked, and you walk out feeling free to move on to more important aspects of your life. And, the best part is the locked room is now forever unlocked.

We all have pain, and we will do almost anything not to feel pain, from drinking or drugging to over- or under-eating, to sexual acting out, and, for some, sadly, even suicide. What no one seems to tell us is what to do with that pain and how to move through the pain, and then what incredible relief and benefits we will derive from unwrapping, looking at, and experiencing that pain, and seeing it for what it is. Think about people's fear before walking across hot coals, and then think about how happy they are after they've finished. It's not just because it's over; it's because they have moved through their fear (hot coals) onto something better (accomplishment).

My friend Jeremy and I discussed how the pain we hold inside of us is like holding onto a bag of rocks. We queried why we hold on to these heavy bags and why we don't just drop them. We have talked about this subject for many hours on many different occasions. Why do it, why not do it? What's the draw, or benefit, to keep holding the rocks? If putting down the bag of rocks is putting down our pain, why is it so hard to do it?

Let's say you take a rock. A substantial one. One that is about ten pounds. Put it in a bag with handles and a strap. Hold it. Hold it with your right hand, and when it gets heavy, switch to your left. When it gets too heavy for your left hand, put the strap on one shoulder, then switch the strap to the other when that gets too heavy. Then maybe hoist the rock up on top of one shoulder, now up on your head, now on top of the other shoulder, and then again back in your hand. Get a backpack and put it in there. When that gets too heavy, switch the backpack to the front and carry it there. When that gets too heavy, get a friend. Ask your friend to hold one handle while you hold the other. After they tire of that, put the rock back on your shoulder. Continue this process for the rest of your life. Or decide to sit with the pain. Again, it is all your choice. You are free to do what you want.

If you decide it's time to drop that bag, I invite you to find a place to be alone for an hour or so. You may want to have some comfort like pillows, blanket, water, writing material, and tissues. You definitely want to be where you will not be disturbed. When it is time, close your eyes, bring up what you know evokes great emotional pain, what holds you back and why, and begin to allow the pain to show itself:

1. Sit with the pain. *(It's not easy, and only you can decide if you're ready.)*
2. Seek out and remember the first time you experienced this pain. *(Who's the cause of it? Where did it happen? What were you doing? How old were you?)*
3. Allow the inner child to cry and cry and wail at the injustice. *(The deeper you go, the better.)*
4. Think of all the reasons why this should not have happened. *(It was wrong. It was not your fault.)*
5. Cry and let the child-you express herself until she is complete. *(Write or draw if you need or want to. Punch the pillow, scream at the top of your lungs. Cry until you are spent, then hug the little one inside. She is deserving of your love.)*
6. And now, let the adult-you decide how this type of thing will be handled from now on, and let the adult-you take care of and

protect the child-you so that this will never, ever happen again. *(Create your new thought pattern of what you will say, and get clear on what you will do to prevent the abusive behavior from happening again. Write it down so it won't be forgotten in moments of upset and confusion.)*

7. Turn your attention from what was (the past) to where and who you want to be from this day forward (future), and don't look back, don't go back, don't allow the negative event to take up real estate in your mind. *(You do not have to forgive nor forget (we'll get to that later). Now is the time for you to decide how the adult-you is taking control and protecting the child-you.)*

Do You Even Realize How Powerful You Are?

It's ok to decide to love that little inner child more than anyone has ever loved her before. As with many of the other subjects I've shared here, it starts off slow, but gains momentum as you learn how to love and care for her. You, the adult-you, is going to protect the child-you from any of that negative stuff happening again. You must go through the pain for it to dissipate, but the reward is worth it. A few minutes of pain and then you get to live the rest of your life freer, happier, calmer, and with more joy, peace, and fulfillment.

I've done this work myself. I've sat with the pain several times. I've had to find the time or take the time. I've had to really feel the emotional pain, along with the tears, the snot, the sobs, the wailing, the rocking. It hurts. Bad. Yet when it's over, and I've hugged myself, and I've finally gone to the bathroom and wiped my face off, I am changed forever. The inner child-me has wanted to express her pain, and when I finally let her, the pain dissipates. She's been heard.

Each time I had come to a place where I knew, deep down inside, that the pain was holding me back, I also somehow sensed I had the strength necessary to get through to the other side. Every time I am blown away, amazed, shocked, and surprised at the level of *relief* I feel when it is over. Not just because it is over, but because of how much pressure and stress has been released from my body. My wish for you is to recognize that you too have the strength to sit with the pain, and then move beyond it—and the promise is that you will never regret it.

What Jessica realized after sitting with the pain was that although she could not forgive the emotional abuse put on her by her father, she did recognize his humanness and was able to see how poorly his parents had treated him while he was growing up. Again, the circumstances hadn't changed, but her understanding of his life had, and seeing his vulnerability as a child and what he had gone through allowed her to shift her feelings. This shift in her awareness and understanding allowed Jessica to be free from the emotional pain and to stop feeling victimized.

She told me, "I can't believe all the pain is just gone. Like that, in one sitting, it just went away." She admitted going through the pain was hard and it hurt, but then, the pain was gone. Like me, her inner child wanted to be seen and heard. Can you see the importance of allowing your inner child to express herself in tears, and just allow the pain to be felt?

The Other Side

Pain is a tough space to be in. You have to really want to move past the pain to do this exercise. You must be willing to find a quiet, safe space, be willing to take yourself to a place of potentially intense emotional discomfort, allow the inner child to cry, wail, and weep. You must be willing to remember when this pain began, and see the injustice of living a life that seems unreasonable, unjust, and unfair.

That's a lot to ask anyone, and I understand that. But what is the alternative? Let's get concrete for a minute. We'll make up the amount of time that we experience emotional pain from the past to be an hour a month (1hr x 12 months = 12 hrs), and let's say it lasts for thirty years, that would be twelve hours a year times thirty years (12 hrs x 30 yrs 360 hrs). That's 360 hours of pain, and counting. You know it's way more than that, but even if it's only half that amount of time, it would equal 180 hours of pain in your life.

If you choose it, this would be a journey inward to the most painful space. It would require you to feel it, experience it, hate it, be pissed about it, cry about it, feel helpless about it, and wail about it. This would be for some number of *minutes*, just minutes, not hours, and not for nothing, but for the pain of your inner child to be seen, heard, valued, and acknowledged. Would it be worth it your emotional pain decreased one percent? Ten percent? 50, or even 100 percent?

The only way to get unstuck from the damage done from your past is to face into the fear. Do what you've never been willing to do before because it is what will set you free. It's what's going to make the difference in your life. It is what is going to allow you to release that substantial rock you've been carrying around. Sit with the pain and then be done with it. Otherwise, you will stay stuck in the old stories you've been telling yourself and others for years.

TAKEAWAYS

- Upsetting events that happen in your current day aren't the triggers; they trigger the triggers from your past.
- Sitting with the pain allows you to drop the bag of rocks so you can have more relief and emotional freedom in your life.

Looking to discovery more of who you are? Please join us in the

Self-Discovery Lab. We're waiting for you.

https://www.facebook.com/groups/selfdiscoverylab

9
Four Steps to Keep Moving Forward

It's where the magic happens.

I'd had so much programming from other well-meaning adults that I had no idea what I wanted or who I was. I'd been searching for meaning in my life for decades. I knew some of what I wanted, like I wanted to help others heal emotionally, I wanted to work with women, and I wanted to share my experiences and knowledge with those who wanted to listen.

Instead, I opted for what many Americans are raised to believe, which is you do something meaningful *after* you become financially secure. That never felt right for me, yet I continued doing it for many years. After walking the 500 miles in Spain, getting certified in training and coaching, quitting my unfulfilling job, and devoting my life to helping others heal is when my life became meaningful to me. But that's me. I have no idea what is meaningful to you because it is different for everyone.

Imagine you have a flashlight. One day the light goes on. You see a path you want to go down. It's dark and unknown. Instead of shining the light out in front where you can go step-by-step and acclimate, you bury the flashlight in your pocket, afraid to move. Your light has been turned on, but doing the unknown is too scary, so you hide your light under drama, stress, and chaos. This way it feels like things are happening, but these are not productive, nor will they get you where you want to go.

Living a meaningful life means you have to pull out that flashlight. You must have courage and confidence to head down an unknown path, and shine the light on everything around you to observe what's going on. You can use this illuminating light to decide if you want to stop and stay where you are or move to a new space, keep your fears or build on your strengths, keep your limiting beliefs or shift to empowering ones, avoid confrontation or challenge the status quo. Any and all of these are choices you get to make.

Four-Steps

A client once told our group about what she learned from the Personal Profile Tool and finding meaning: "I did this tool for myself. I saw my strengths and weaknesses side by side. I saw things about myself that I've never realized before. I kept moving forward until I really knew myself. Every aspect of my life has changed. It's better. I no longer go to work feeling like the stupidest or weakest person on earth. I feel my strength. I know where I want to go, and I'm happy and grateful every day. What's interesting is the more I learn about myself, the more I want to learn."

I was like this too. In the beginning, this was hard work. I had so much programming from others that I had no idea who I was, or what I wanted to do. I can tell you what others wanted me to do; what they felt I should do, shouldn't do, must do, can't do, better do. No matter what I did, some liked it and some didn't. I was on perpetual overwhelm. It's no wonder I felt confused about whether I was doing the right thing or not, no wonder frustration, numbness, and internal anger filled my life. Trying to please others and all the conflicting information is exhausting.

I began to understand others would tell me what they wanted me to do because it made *them* feel better, but it didn't necessarily make *me* feel better, and often it made me feel worse. I wanted to live my life according to what I wanted, what I needed and what was important for me.

Little by little, I began to make tiny changes, and from those tiny changes came bigger ones. And from the bigger ones came some incredible ones. Actions and thoughts that changed my conscious choices in ways that have allowed me to live a happier and freer life. I saw what I had written about myself on the Personal Profile Tool, and I knew that in order to make changes, I would need some sort of guide. Over time I saw a pattern. I realized that I would repeat these same four steps in both large and small ways:

1. I decided what I wanted (*I've done this many times and continue to do it.*)
2. I wrote it down (*The black-and-white visual is important for your mind to see.*)
3. I made a plan (*I knew what needed to happen for me to get to my desired result.*)
4. I took action (*This is the most critical step - keep moving forward.*)

Allow me to showcase one of the large ways:
It took me thirty-six days of about six to eight hours per day of walking to backpack the Camino in Spain. At rough calculation I took over 2 million steps to get where I wanted to go. Would I have gotten there if I had quit? Of course not. I kept going, and even though sometimes it was tough, sometimes slow, and I even sustained an injury, I'm proud to say I got to my destination. In this case, here was my initial four-step plan:
1. I decided what I wanted to do (*backpack the Camino in Spain*).
2. I wrote it down (*on paper, in my phone, on my calendar, at home, at work*).
3. I made a plan (*where I'd be and when, and I ended up having to change it several times, and that's okay, it happens*).
4. I took action (*again and again and again, each day for many months prior to going and each day while I was there*).

Making change that leads to meaning and fulfilment is a step-by-step process to get you where you want to go. Remember we talked about the brain understanding steps, or processes, and will comply with them, about the brain having the RAS (Reticular Activating System) so it will allow in what you focus on, and that the brain loves to learn? You may or may not realize it but your choices follow neural pathways. You can choose to follow the neural pathways that keep you where you are (old ruts) or you can jump the bank and follow the new ones you decide is a better fit for your current life.

And here's the best part - you are the one who makes the choices of where you are going to take yourself. You do not need anyone else's permission or acceptance to live your life the way you know is best for you. You only need to give permission to yourself.

Your Comfort Zone

This same four-step process holds true for all the goals you have written down. It is also what you can use for each of the smaller stepping stones along the way. If you feel tingles inside of your body, this is wonderful news. It's because you know you'll be moving out of your comfort zone, and the inner you is excited. Your ego, however, might be freaking out a little and feeling as if it is going to die. It's not going to die, and the world is not going to end. It's just uncomfortable until your brain gets familiar with this new way of thinking. For example, think about hearing a funny joke. The first time you hear it, it's funny. Maybe the second and third time too. But after hearing it again, it's not so funny anymore because your brain has expanded. It has gotten used to this info. The same holds true for any possible discomfort your ego might be feeling.

I wrote a silly little poem that I'll share with you. At first, my ego was freaking out a little, telling me that the poem is not good enough and people might dismiss it. I've named my ego, Freak-out Fred. When Fred starts to freak out, I'm give him a minute and then continue with my 4-Step plan. I advocate that it's okay to be bad at something you are trying to get better at, so I'm going to be vulnerable here and share this poem. about living in my comfort zone:

> No wonder things weren't happening,
> no wonder my life was slow.
> I was living in a circle,
> with no real place to go.
>
> Round and round I found myself,
> Always curving right,
> until one day I saw something new,
> like someone shown a light.
>
> It's time to leave this comfort zone,
> places I've repeatedly been,
> and seek new adventures out there,
> it's where the magic happens.
>
> So now I wonder what it will take,
> To get my ass in gear,
> To choose to live a life of love,
> instead of living in fear.

It's okay to feel the fear, but don't let fear stop you. It's ok to feel a little uncomfortable but don't let it control you. It's ok to be where you are, just keep moving forward.

I don't know what you think of my poem, but it's ok, because I don't need another person to validate me anymore. I have learned that it's ok to validate myself. It doesn't matter if my poem was good or bad to anyone else, it's mine and it was fun to create it. That's the important part, and that's how I live a more fulfilled life. Living outside my comfort zone allows my cells to feel alive. Life is fun, exciting and more fulfilling when I live this way.

Abraham Maslow said, "In any given moment, we have two options, to step forward into growth or to step back into safety."

A Voice for the Horses

Here's a story when I stepped forward in growth, even though I didn't realize it at the time. It has since, been a profound moment in time I look back at repeatedly.

A few years ago, I was invited to participate in a team-building event, with horses. It's called equine assisted learning. I'm a city girl and had only been around horses a couple times in my life, so I was super stoked to participate.

For Challenge #1 we were given two rules: No touching the horse and no talking, not even to each other. As a team we were to move the horses from the front of the arena to the back. With only this for instructions we were all a bit confused about how to get this done. After about twenty minutes of nonverbal struggle, we somehow got the horses where we wanted them. Success. We all went to the whiteboard at the front and discussed our challenges, strengths, and weaknesses. At first, it was pretty cool.

Challenge #2 was more difficult and the rules were different: no touching the horses, this time we could talk, and we were to use available items lying around the arena to create a pathway for one of the horses to go down. We used some bright blue 55-gallon plastic barrels and placed ten-foot long by three-inch round white PVC piping across the tops to create a makeshift feeder-line. For a challenge for the horse, we put a 3-foot round ball in the middle of the pathway. We were to consider ourselves successful if we could get the horse to go all the way through the nearly 25-foot long feeder-line.

Everyone was pumped from our previous success. Surely, we could do this. The Challenge began and we decided on two of us being on the left of the feeder-line and two on the right, and I went down to the other end. At first all was going well, but then the horse got to the ball and stopped. She did not feel comfortable anymore and began to look for a way out. Down at the end I tried calling the horse (that doesn't work, btw).

The others began acting weird, like they began feeding off each other's energy. I watched as their momentum picked up.

Getting the horse to continue and go in the direction they wanted her to go seemed paramount. They began screaming and yelling at the horse. Someone was clapping their hands at her and waving their arms, another whistled loudly. So much confusion. And, if that wasn't enough, another grabbed a couple of long wiggly styrofoam float toys and began vigorously waving them in the horse's face attempting to get her to head back down the feeder-line. I felt like I was watching a horrible movie in slow motion. My mouth opened, my eyes wide, my brow furrowed, and shaking my head I said, "Nooooo," but no one heard me. They were wrapped up in their own world.

As the horse's head turned one way and then another looking for a way out, for a split second she looked directly into my eyes. It felt as if she were begging me to help.

"NOOOOOooooooo," I spoke louder this time. Still no one stopped. They could not hear over their own thoughts. I could see the horse was miserable and wanted to be left alone. The humans were almost in a frenzy trying to get this horse to turn where they wanted her to go.

"S-T-O-P!" I screamed. Shocked, they stopped, turned and looked at me. And the second they did, the horse knocked the PVC piping down and took off to the back of the arena, as far from us as possible.

Frustrated and in disbelief of what I had just witnessed, I angrily said to the participant who had flailed the funoodles in the horse's face "Don't ever do that again!" Turning to the owner, I said, "I don't like this. I don't like what we did. I don't like how we treated this horse. I want out." My voice was strong and absolute.

Surprisingly, I was met with a bit of chiding where others didn't feel like my point was valid. I heard statements indicating that we weren't doing anything wrong, she's just a horse, why am I bothered, this is just an exercise in team building, what's my problem, and so on.

Irritated, the only man, the one who was flailing the

funoodles in the horse's face, said with a little too much disdain, "We had a challenge to complete." As if that made it ok.

"We had a challenge, yes," I said, "but to what end? Do you really feel that it was okay to shove items into the horse's face just so that she would do what you wanted?"

"I think we were accomplishing our goal," said one lady, who, surprisingly, happened to be a therapist.

"I think the only thing we were accomplishing here is to prove that humans can be assholes," I responded. "Were you not aware of how uncomfortable the horse became as we continued to literally shove our desire in her face? Does how she feel have no meaning, as long as we reach our goal?" During all of this, the owner of the horses was quiet, watching the interplay between me and her other guests.

I could no longer be part of this. I had to leave. I cried for the first thirty miles back to my house. I was in much emotional distress.

About three hours after I had gotten home, the owner called. I almost didn't answer, but I'm glad I did. During our conversation she asked if I remembered the horses coming by us and the large, male horse standing between me and that guy. I said I did vaguely. I noticed they were there, but I was so caught up in delivering my message it didn't register to me that the horses assembling amongst us meant anything. She told me the horses knew I was speaking for them, and their presence meant they agreed. I'm not sure I understand that, but I felt really happy that she told me, and even more happy when she told me there will never be any more funoodles or abusive actions allowed again.

Although it took a couple of years before I realized it, the challenge reminded me of when I was being abused and not having anyone to stand up for me. Standing up for the horses made me realize that I have a voice, and the adult-me is capable of standing up for the child-me. It felt powerful standing my ground. It was also interesting that I wasn't letting any of those other people bully me into stepping back, especially the angry man. Somehow, I knew beyond a shadow of a doubt, that what I was saying was so important that I didn't really care if they agreed with me or not. I wasn't trying to get anyone to like me. I wasn't playing small. I played big, and full out, and I am proud of what I did, even though none of these thoughts were going through my mind at the time.

In that one afternoon, having the moral courage to speak up about what felt like injustice, changed lives, both human lives and the lives of the horses. As more people find their inner strength, stand up and speak out, there will be more ripples.

So, what is moral courage? As defined by Jack Russell of the Center of Self-Sustaining Leadership, it is *"doing the right thing, for the right people, at the right time."* I stood up for what I believed in regardless of what others thought of me, or said to me, or how nasty they acted toward me. I just knew it was the right thing to do, and I did it.

I will warn you, though. There are those who are not going to like you standing up, taking charge of your life and speaking out, especially if it shines a negative light on them, or if they feel their control over you is being challenged. Others might express their fear of you changing and will want you to go back to the way you've always been. There could be "don't rock the boat" attitudes, people wondering what's wrong with you, and others might get downright angry with you. You may experience some trying to confuse you because you making new decisions is going to change and shift the status quo to something new. Doing things differently does take courage, but it is the road to your freedom. If you are looking for some comfort or reassurance, you can join my facebook group for support (see Thank You page, back of book).

I can assure you moral courage is far easier than the adversity you've already been through. Using it and getting used to it takes new brain muscle. This is so healthy for your brain because you'll build new neural pathways. Just like any other muscle you exercise it will get stronger and easier to use. As soon as you've gone through it, it will be in the realm of the brain that the brain understands (aka safety).

Do the right thing for the right people at the right time and treat yourself with the same love, dignity, and respect that you do for others. As you put your foot lovingly down, stand in your strength, and people understand that you mean what you say (even if they argue, fuss, and fight) is you, loving you. And I promise you, purpose and meaningfulness will not only come into your life, it will become your way of life.

TAKEAWAYS

- Use the 4-Step Plan (Decide it, Write it, Plan it, Act on it) to keep you moving forward.
- Use your voice and be proud of your Moral Courage (doing the right thing, for the right people (person, animan), at the right time).

10
Is Today the Day?

What's the payoff?

What if you knew, in the core of your soul, that this exact moment would mark the point in time where you stepped up and chose to change your life in a truly transformational way? What if making this commitment becomes the key that finally unlocks the door to releasing all that inner emotional pain forever?

One of the main reasons I think it took me so many years to get past the pain is because I had a vested interest in staying stuck in that painful place. I know this sounds counterintuitive, but it is amazing what we do when we are not aware of it.

When I was yelling about something my dad did, I got something that I considered to be love. People would love me by listening, nodding, furrowing their brow at the insanity, shaking their head, and feeling sorry for me. And that was powerful. I was getting attention, which was something I wasn't getting at home, and that attention fueled me.

When I was angry about something, I considered my anger to be my dad's fault, so by raging about it, I found that other people would seemingly enjoy my rage and egg me on. It was as if they were living vicariously through me. They had anger too but couldn't show it, but I could, and because of that they wanted me to be angry, basically, for them. I didn't know that's what was happening, and I don't think they did either, but it was. Their encouragement for me to continue being angry was another benefit—or so I thought.

I found that while I was feeling the pain and wallowing in it, I felt justified in hating. Nothing felt like my fault, and I could blame all my problems on my dad. Sure, he created the mess, but after three-plus decades of being out of his house, plus the last eight of those years he was dead, I was still bemoaning my childhood and placing all the blame on him - I mean it was, after all, still his fault, right?

I remember one day a thought went through my head that stopped me dead in my tracks. It went something like this: "He's dead and you are still blaming him that your life sucks. Isn't that a little like you are now your own abuser?" I'm...my...own...abuser? I could see how I was using him as an excuse to continue having great inner pain and turmoil. It still blows me away when I think about it. This was another key turning point for me.

I share this because it's important to see that sometimes there might be a payoff for holding on to the pain. If any of these scenarios feel familiar, take some time to evaluate what the reason is for you. Like we've talked about, we can only change what we are aware of.

Arguing for Your Beliefs

I can teach you what I know, and what I know works, but in the end, the only person who can get the results you are searching for is you. You are the only person who can stop staying stuck. If you choose to keep your reasons or your fears, don't want to feel your feelings, don't think anything is your responsibility, or think you aren't someone unless you are miserable, you get to stay where you are. Argue for your limiting beliefs, and you get to keep them.

11
Learn, Practice, Progress

When I moved into an apartment after living in a house, I missed having my garden, especially fresh vegetables and herbs. I decided I wanted to have a container garden on my balcony. I'd seen these types of gardens before but wondered what other information I needed to know—such as if a particular type of soil was needed, what depth certain roots grow, whether chemicals from the plastic planters would leach into the soil, and therefore into my food, and so on.

I bought a book that provided me this sort of information, and I started reading it. As I got to the last page, I closed the book, and looked over at my balcony. I still had lots to do. However, as I read the book, I had begun gathering many of the tools and supplies I needed to get my garden growing.

I knew that if I gave it time and nurtured it, my garden would not only grow but thrive. The same principles apply to what you have learned in this book. Self-discovery is like having the basic gardening tools. Deeper self-knowing is the container. The willingness to learn and grow is the soil. Observing your patterns will fertilize your thoughts, and the blooms will bring meaningfulness into your life. Just like a garden, your inner growth requires nurturing.

Moving forward goes beyond simply reading the words in this or any book. It requires putting what you've learned into practice and actively choosing to take action. Life itself is a learning laboratory, rich with lessons that must be experienced firsthand. This journey involves deciding whether to let old, limiting thoughts prevail or to champion new, empowering ideas. Remember, your ego might resist change, equating it to a kind of death. But rest assured, while a negative thought pattern or a disempowering belief may fall away, you will not. This process is about growth and transformation, not loss.

As with most everything we've ever learned in life ...

(1) we learn something new; (2) we practice it; (3) we grow, or progress.

REFERENCES

Gary Chapman, *The 5 Love Languages: The Secret to Love That Lasts.*

Lynne Forrest, *Guiding Principles for Life Beyond Victim Consciousness* (also an article, "The Three Faces of Victim").

Stephen B. Karpman, MD, *A Game Free Life: The definitive book on the Drama Triangle and Compassion Triangle by the originator and author.*

Marshall Rosenberg, PhD, *Nonviolent Communication: A Language of Life.*

Don Miguel Ruiz, *The Four Agreements: A Practical Guide to Personal Freedom (a Toltec Wisdom Book).*

Jack Russell and Glenda Otto from the Center for Self-Sustaining Leadership

ACKNOWLEDGMENTS

To the woman who started me on the path of awareness, I want to acknowledge Nohemy Bradley. She has been a faithful friend and has loved me unconditionally my entire life, and I can tell you that has been one tough feat. She is one of the most powerful mentors I've known, and I'm thankful to have her loving guidance. She is the one who originally brought consciousness into my life, and for that I am forever grateful. Nohemy, I don't know how I would have gotten through life without you. You are a precious gem.

I want to thank another essential soul in my life, Jeremy Aultman. Through countless hours of discussions, he has been there for me. He has listened to me laugh, cry, shout, scream, blame, shame, and complain on a million different topics, and he's also helped me become consciously aware in ways I could never have imagined. I don't know how I would have grown so much without him. Jeremy, from the bottom of my heart, I thank you for all you have given me and for not allowing the bag of rocks to be too easy to carry nor too hard to put down.

Thank you to Paul and Pat Owens for their kind and generous friendship, and for the quote in chapter 7 about "the love of power being overshadowed by the power of love."

A special thank you goes to my longtime friend and confidante, Amy Baskin, for her loving, caring, ever present, unwavering encouragement and support for all that I have done and continue to do. I also want to acknowledge the many hours she has spent listening to me, and for the feedback, suggestions, trust, kindness, and love, which have been invaluable. Thank you also, Amy, for trusting me to present to your students, which has been the catalyst for me to move forward into a place of confidence in speaking in front of people and, ultimately, to this book. Creating and presenting the master class on "The Importance of Intentions" was a missing piece of the puzzle. I now feel unstoppable, and I thank you.

Tons of appreciation also go to the Center for Self-Sustaining Leadership. I want to acknowledge the personalized coaching and training that I've received for this work from the founders, Jack Russell and Glenda Otto. My personal connection to you both has been heartfelt and so appreciated. I look forward to many more years of connection and participation.

Much appreciation and thanks to Ariana Drown and Alicia Ayles who helped with research, coaching, suggestions and quotes, and for allowing me into their lives with open arms.

And last but certainly not least, to Chellie Campbell, creator of the Financial Stress Reduction® Workshop who taught me that I am more valuable than a paycheck and that the limit for financial abundance is as high as I wish to make it. Chellie, your ripples have a lasting effect and reach further than you could ever know.

REFERENCES

Doyen S, Klein O, Pichon CL, Cleeremans A. *Behavioral priming: it's all in the mind, but whose mind?* PLoS One. 2012;7(1):e29081. doi: 10.1371/journal.pone.0029081. Epub 2012 Jan 18. PMID: 22279526; PMCID: PMC3261136. National Library of Medicine. https://www.ncbi.nlm.nih.gov/pmc/articles/PMC3261136/

Forrest, Lynne, and Eileen Meagher. (2011) *Guiding Principles for Life Beyond Victim Consciousness*

Karpman, MD, Stephen. (2020) *The Karpman Drama Triangle Explained: A Guide for Coaches, Managers, Trainers, Therapists – and Everybody Else*

Rosenberg, Ph.D., Marshall B. (2015) *Nonviolent Communication: A Language of Life.* 3rd ed. PuddleDancer Press.

Russell, Jack and Glenda Otto. (2023) *Self-Sustaining Leadership® Essential Skills and Frameworks* (2nd ed.)

ABOUT THE AUTHOR

Debbie Pearson is an author, coach, visionary, and healer dedicated to helping women embrace their inner voice and reconnect with their inner child, leading to a life filled with joy, fulfillment, and freedom.

In 2015, at the pinnacle of her career, Debbie found herself adrift, seeking her life's purpose and grappling with unresolved emotional pain and anger. This set her on a quest to discover more of who she authentically is. She decided to backpack the 500-mile trek across Spain called El Camino de Santiago. With each step, she gained deeper insights into her role in the world and what mattered most to her.

Since completing her transformative journey, Debbie has accumulated numerous hours in conventional and non-conventional training. In late 2016, she made her move. She quit her job, all her possessions, and embarked on a new path—one that would bring the personal fulfillment she had been looking for. Today, she is an entrepreneur, owner of SelfDiscoveryCircle.com (a membership site for women only), on social media, a podcaster, and is writing her next book.

Debbie's expertise lies in fostering deep self-awareness, unlocking inner voices, nurturing one's inner child, and gently releasing emotional pain. Her real-world experiences, extensive background, and genuine, grounded approach make her an ideal guide for anyone on the thrilling, rewarding, and sometimes daunting journey of self-transformation and discovery.

She can be reached at Deb@DebbiePearson.com

THANK YOU FOR READING THIS

I have some freebies for you.

FREE INTERACTIVE, SUPPORTIVE GROUP FOR WOMEN, JUST LIKE YOU

Discover more together in the Lab! Join our free, private Facebook group for women, where we explore exciting new topics every month through trainings, activities, guest sessions, and more. Join us and be inspired!

https://www.facebook.com/groups/selfdiscoverylab

Get the free Personal Profile Tool (and other free stuff) at https://www.debbiesfreebies.com/

THANK YOU FOR POSTING YOUR REVIEW ON AMAZON!

www.ingramcontent.com/pod-product-compliance
Lightning Source LLC
Chambersburg PA
CBHW070854050426
42453CB00012B/2189